# A Descriptive Account

— OF —

# BERWICK-ON-TWEED.

ILLUSTRATED.

W. T. PIKE & CO.,
*Publishers*,
GRAND PARADE, BRIGHTON.

First published in Great Britain 1995
by Berwick-upon-Tweed Borough Council,
Wallace Green, Berwick-upon-Tweed, TD15 1ED.

© Additional text by Linda Bankier 1995.

Reprinted from the 1894 edition,
first published by W.T. Pike & Co., Brighton.

© Additional photographs by Jim Walker F.R.P.S. 1995.

The right of Linda Bankier to be identified as author of this work has been asserted by her in accordance with the Copyright, Designs and Patents Act 1988.

ISBN    0 9526738 0 0

Printed by How and Blackhall,
77 Marygate, Berwick-upon-Tweed, TD15 1BB.

# FOREWORD

Originally called "A Descriptive Account of Berwick-on-Tweed Illustrated", this publication produced by W.T. Pike and Company of Brighton, first appeared in 1894. Since then a reprint of the trade section was reproduced in 1972 by the late Robert Bell. However, as 1994 was the centenary of the original publication, it seemed appropriate to republish the book in its original form and include updates on all the premises featured in 1894. To make the publication both an historical and visual record of 1994 as well as 1894, photographs have been added of the premises today which were taken by Jim Walker F.R.P.S. As far as possible, the photographs have been taken from the same position as the originals.

Information on the premises and their use in the past 100 years has been gathered from various sources including old trade directories, newspapers, shop owners and people in the town. I am particularly indebted to the Berwick historian Francis Cowe, and Eric Middlemis, from Blackburn and Price who provided me with a lot of information and many a story about the premises in the past.

On researching this book, I have found it interesting that there are only a few sites where the original 1894 buildings have been totally demolished (Messrs James R. Black and Company in Love Lane; George Black, boiler makers in Tweedmouth and James Brough's premises in Bridge Street) Most of the original buildings still remain although many have been modified beyond recognition at street level. Often it was only possible to positively identify a building by looking at the layout of the windows on the first floor level.

The use of most of the buildings featured in the original publication has changed considerably in the past 100 years with the exception of the Kings Arms, Hen and Chickens Hotel and Paxton and Purves (but no longer owned by the family). Another business still survives from the original publication - Ralph Holmes and Sons - although it has moved to the shop next door in Bridge Street.

As the original publication was selective in the premises it featured (probably those who were willing to pay), obviously the updates can only give a limited picture of shops and their appearance in 1994. Time does not stand still and this is particularly true in respect of shops and shop fronts. Often shop fronts change or businesses move from one premises to another without us even registering that anything has changed. However, hopefully this present publication will at least give future readers a permanent record of shop fronts in 1994 and perhaps it will lead to a further update in another 100 years !

Linda Bankier
Borough Archivist

# BERWICK-ON-TWEED.

IT is no exaggeration to say that Berwick is one of the most interesting towns in the United Kingdom. In fact, we could not name six others which have such a stirring history, and certainly none which has in the past enjoyed such an unique position and such peculiar privileges. In fact, for a parallel with the Berwick of four hundred years ago, we have to look either to the independent cities of Northern Italy, or the towns upon the Baltic which made up the Hanseatic League. Berwick possessed in the matter of its government privileges which no other town in Britain has ever enjoyed. The "Berwick Bounds" were constituted by Henry IV. an entirely independent district with a Government separate from that of either England or Scotland, and a little Court of its own embracing a Lord Chancellor, a Lord Chamberlain and other officials. In fact, right up to the middle of the last century, the reign of George II, no Act of Parliament applied to Berwick unless the town was specially mentioned in that act: while the peculiar powers of life and death granted to the borough by James I., remained in force until they were taken away by the Limitation of Jurisdiction of Quarter Sessions Act of 1842. The "Berwick Bounds" mentioned above, the legal style of which is the "County of the Town and Borough of Berwick-upon-Tweed," extends along the coast northwards from the mouth of the Tweed three and a half miles, and about the same distance inland, its limit being at Lamberton in Berwickshire. This latter place was once as notorious as Gretna Green for Scottish weddings. Until the year 1310 Berwick was

W. Green]      TOWN HALL FROM WEST STREET.      [Berwick.

*Published by* W. T. PIKE AND CO., *Grand Parade, Brighton.*

in the Archdeaconry of Lothian and Diocese of St. Andrews, but at that date it was transferred by Edward II. to the diocese of Durham, and so it continued until 1882, when the See of Newcastle-on-Tyne was created.

That Berwick is a town of the highest antiquity there is no doubt. Antiquaries are agreed that a bridge spanned the Tweed here even in pre-Roman days; and that this bridge, which was repaired successively by the Romans, Saxons and Danes, was the one which and so it remained until after the rebellion against William II., when it was joined to the Palatinate of Durham, under Bishop Walcher. Previous to this Eadulf, one of the Saxon Earls of Northumbria, had sold Berwick and the northern half of the Earldom, known as Bernicia, to Malcolm II. of Scotland. The district was, however, handed over to Henry II. in accordance with the treaty of Falaise (1174) made between that monarch and William the Lion, of Scotland, who was then a prisoner in his hands. The

W. Green]  THE PARISH CHURCH.  [Berwick.

was carried away by the floods in 1199. Leland derives the name of Berwick from *Aber-wick*, " the town at the mouth of the river." During the 8th and 9th centuries it first began to gain importance as a frontier town between the kingdom of Northumbria and that of Scotland. Boece, writing in the 16th century, says that it was here that the Danes landed in 867 under Hubba. When Ealdred made himself absolute King of England, he drove out Eric the titular king of Northumbria, and placed the great northern province under the government of earls; town, however, did not long remain in the hands of the English, for fifteen years later it was sold to the Scottish king by Richard Cœur-de-Lion, who was raising money in every quarter to equip his expedition to Palestine. The price paid by Scotland for the vassalage of the town was 10,000 marks, or £6,666 13s. 4d. A quarter of a century later King John, returning from his unsuccessful invasion of Scotland, burned Berwick, upon his retreat; and the town was almost entirely rebuilt by the Scots. At the same time the town was still regarded in a manner as debateable ground, upon which English and Scotch alike could meet upon a common footing, and several important conferences were held here between representatives of the two nations. In 1235 a very pacific function was performed here, for in the church of St. Lawrence, Gilbert Marshall, the powerful English Earl of Pembroke, was married to the sister of Alexander II. of Scotland.

In 1291, Berwick was the scene of a most important conference, for here sat the 104 English and Scottish Commissioners who were to decide between the rival claims of Robert Bruce and John Balliol to the throne of Scotland. Guided no doubt by the paramount influence of Edward I., the Commissioners decided in favour of Balliol, who for five years was nominal King of Scotland. When in 1296, goaded by continual insults upon the part of his "paramount-lord," the King of England, Balliol tried to assert his right as an independent monarch, and was promptly dethroned, Berwick was stormed and taken by the English. This was one of the most sanguinary experiences ever suffered by the frontier town, for it is said that nearly eight thousand of the inhabitants of Berwick were slain during the siege and storming of the fortress. In the same year Edward I. held a Parliament here, and received the homage of the leading Scottish nobles. In 1297 the Scottish hero, William Wallace, captured the town, but was unable to take the castle, and was forced to retreat.

In 1306, in the absence of the Earl of Fife, in England, his sister Isabel (Comyn), Countess of Buchan, crowned Robert Bruce at Scone. Enraged at this act, Edward I. imprisoned the Countess in an iron cage in Berwick Castle, where she remained for some years. Edward II. was frequently here during the Scottish wars, both before and after Bannockburn. In 1318, four years after the latter battle, the Scots took Berwick, and Bruce considerably strengthened it. In 1321 the marriage took place here between Joan, the infant sister of Edward III., and David, the young son of Bruce. On the death of

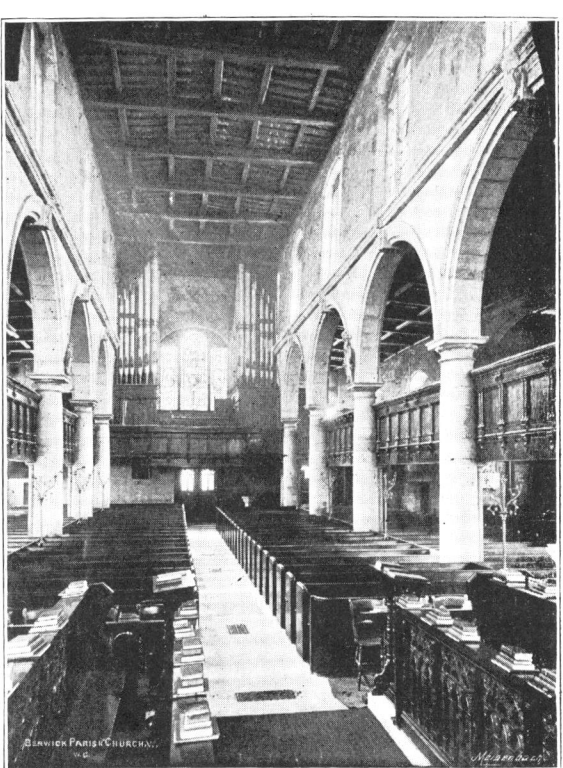

*W. Green*]   INTERIOR OF PARISH CHURCH.   [*Berwick*.

4  BERWICK-ON-TWEED—ILLUSTRATED.

Bruce, the war between Scotland and England broke out afresh, and Edward III. besieged and captured Berwick in 1333. It is said that at the siege of Berwick, upon this occasion, cannon were for the first time used in actual warfare.

For the next one hundred and fifty years, the period of the most sanguinary of the Border feuds, when the Douglasses led the Scotch and the Percys the English, Berwick was continually changing hands. It was finally annexed to the English crown of Edward IV., in 1482. During the Wars of the Roses, the town seems to have been neutral. It is said to be the place where Queen Margaret and her son Edward embarked for France in 1462, after their romantic adventures subsequent to the disastrous defeat at Hexham. Another Queen Margaret, the daughter of Henry VII., and wife of the unfortunate James IV. of Scotland, was here twice. First when welcomed by the townspeople upon the occasion of her wedding, and again after the death of her husband upon Flodden Field (1513). By a treaty made between Edward VI. and Mary Queen of Scots, in 1551, Berwick was declared neutral ground, independent of either England or Scotland, and so it remained until the crowns of both kingdoms were united upon the head of James VI. of Scotland and I. of England. It was at Berwick that James made his state entry into the realm he had inherited. From this date the importance of Berwick naturally began to decline. Charles I. was here in 1633 upon his way to be crowned at Edinburgh : and again in 1639 with the army he had gathered for his expedition against the Scottish Covenanters—an expedition which was brought to an end by the " Pacification of Berwick." During the great Civil War the townspeople fortified Berwick for the protection of themselves and their trade, and took up neutral ground between the contending parties. The town was, however, taken in 1647 by Sir Marmaduke Langdale, on behalf of the King, and surrendered a year later to Cromwell, in person. The Lord Protector was here again in 1650 on his way to Dunbar.

In 1703, in consequence of the passing of the Act of Security by the Scottish Parliament, and in anticipation of the troubles that might arise therefrom, Berwick was again garrisoned by the English. During the Jacobite rebellions of the last century, Berwick was curiously enough left alone. In 1804,

W. Green]  THE OLD BRIDGE.  [Berwick.

during the Napoleonic War, the town of Berwick voted £1,000 towards the national defences, and showed that the old martial spirit had not died out in the old frontier town, by raising two companies of Volunteers.

Having thus briefly sketched the eventful history of Berwick, we will proceed to give our readers some account of the town as it appears to-day, its chief architectual features, and its commercial and industrial resources.

The town is now governed by a Mayor, six Aldermen, and eighteen Councillors, whose jurisdiction also includes the district of Tweedmouth and Spittal on the south side of the Tweed. This body has done much to develop the town. There is a splendid water supply, reputed to be the purest in England, and the town is well lighted by gas; the works, which were constituted under a deed of settlement, December, 1844, are the property of a company incorporated under the Company's Act, 11th of October, 1893.

The most interesting architectural feature of the town lies in the remains of the castle, whose history has been substantially the history of Berwick. There was a fortress here from the earliest date in our history, and we have records of its re-building by David I. of Scotland, between the year 1124-53. When the town came into the possession of Henry II. in 1174, he again rebuilt David's stronghold, and his structure was considerably added to at subsequent periods. Queen Elizabeth, especially, did much to strengthen both the castle and the fortifications of the town. The castle occupied an eminence at the north-east of the town, but most of the buildings have now disappeared. The grand old Bell Tower, in three stories, however, still stands, and from it the curfew, until recent times, was rung each night at

W. Green]  THE NEW BRIDGE.  [Berwick.

eight o'clock. This tower had once a beacon upon its summit, which was used to warn the people of the surrounding district of the approach of marauding parties.

We have already alluded to the fact that a bridge was here in the Roman, Saxon and Danish periods, and that it was washed away by the floods in 1199. It was rebuilt by William the Lion; but the present bridge between Berwick and Tweedmouth dates from 1609—34. It is a magnificent structure of stone, 1,164 feet in length and 17 feet wide, and is erected with 15 arches. The railway viaduct, the Royal

Border Bridge, is about half-a-mile higher up the Tweed. It is the property of the North Eastern Railway Company, and was opened by the Queen in 1850. t consists of 28 spans of 61 feet 6 inches each, and is built of stone and brick. Its length is 2,160 feet, somewhat narrow, they are well paved and well lighted.

Berwick is a port of considerable consequence. In 1848 it was re-limited, its boundaries being S. Abbs Head, on the north (the limit of the port of Leith),

W. Green]          WALLACE GREEN CHURCH.          [Berwick.

and breadth, including parapets, 24 feet. Its greatest height is 126 feet 6 inches above the river. The engineer of this bridge was Robert Stephenson, the designer of the Menai Bridge.

There are two main entrances into the town. The and Alnwater on the south (the limit of the port of Shields). There is a splendid pier, for the protection of shipping, begun in 1810, and completed at an outlay of £50,000. It is built of solid masonry.

The Parish Church dedicated to Holy Trinity is an

W. Green]          THE RAMPARTS.          [Berwick

one from the south is over the old bridge; while the one from the north is by Castle Gate, through the Scotch Gate—along a noble and wide thoroughfare about a quarter of a mile in length. Although some of the streets branching off to the right and left are edifice of stone in the Italian style. It was originally erected in 1648; and restored in 1855. At the latter date it was enlarged by the addition of a chancel, and the sum of about £4,000 spent upon its restoration. It was again restored in 1879 at a cost of upwards of £2,000.

As seen now the building forms a parallelogram, ninety feet in length and sixty-four in breadth. The interior is divided by arcades, of five arches, into a nave, with aisles of equal length. There is a beautifully stained east window erected as a memorial to the Rev. Joseph Barnes, who was for fifty years vicar of the parish. He died 5th December, 1855. Most of the other windows are stained, and serve as memorials to prominent local residents and donors. The pulpit and reading-desk are of oak. The former, which is finely panelled, was removed from the original Church, at St. Mary's Gate. It is said to be the pulpit from which John Knox preached, during two years. The west window is one of great beauty. It was presented to the Church by Sir Dudley Coutts Marjoribanks, M.P., afterwards Lord Tweedmouth. It was removed from the Church of Whitchurch, in Middlesex, which was formerly the private Chapel of the "Princely Chandos" of Canon Park. The Church contains many tablets; while the churchyard, which covers two acres, is crowded with tomb-stones. John Smithson, who was vicar of the Church (1664-72) was executed for the murder of his wife.

St. Mary's Church, in Castle Gate, was erected in 1858, through the munificence of Captain Charles Gordon, and cost £3,000. The building is of Ashlar stone, and is in the Lancet style. It consists of a chancel, nave, transepts, north vestry and small tower. The three lancets in the east contain some fine stained glass windows, and other windows are stained.

The Roman Catholic Church, dedicated to Our Blessed Lady and St. Cuthbert, in Ravensdown, is a building of stone, erected in 1829. The Free Church of Scotland has a chapel here, erected in 1719. Other Nonconformist sects are represented by handsome places of worship, liberally supported by their respective congregations.

The Wallace Green Church was opened in June, 1859. It is of pleasing design and has a well decorated interior with seating accommodation for 1,200 persons. It contains a memorial tablet and a stained glass window in memory of the late Principal Cairns who presided at this church for over thirty years.

The Cemetery is situated one mile from the town,

W. Green]   INTERIOR OF WALLACE GREEN CHURCH.   [Berwick.

upon the Edinburgh road. It covers an area of nine acres, and is very beautifully laid out with shrubs, etc. There are two mortuary chapels in the gothic style. There is a Burial Board of nine members which have control of it.

The Town Hall stands in the middle of the street, at the east end of St. Mary's Gate, or High Street, as it is now generally called. It was erected between the years 1756-61, James Dodds being the architect. It is a very handsome building, and is surmounted by a graceful tower 150 feet in height.

in part preserved in the Barracks, which are situated upon the Parade. Here are the head-quarters of the famous Border Regiment. The buildings, which were erected in 1712, are very extensive, and form a handsome block. They are in the form of a quadrangle measuring 217 feet by 121 feet. There is, too, a coast-guard station near King's Mount, formed in 1879.

The Corn Exchange, which is situated at the foot of Hide Hill, near Sandgate, is a spacious building of stone in the Gothic style, opened in 1858.

The Cattle Market, which is of great importance to

W. Green]　　　　EXCAVATION AT HOLY ISLAND PRIORY.　　　　[Berwick.

Berwick boasts an excellent Dispensary and Infirmary, founded in 1814. The present building was erected in 1874. The institution, which is carrying on a very valuable work, is supported almost entirely by voluntary contributions. In High Street is the Literary and Scientific Institute, in connection with which is the Art School, conducted by Mr. Wallace. There is a well supported Subscription Room in Palace Green.

The ancient military importance of Berwick is still

Berwick, is situated in Castlegate, a market is held on every Saturday, and is largely attended by farmers from the surrounding districts.

Opposite to the Town Hall, in High Street, is situated the Fish Market. This market is very abundantly supplied, the fishing industry being one of great importance in Berwick.

Like most ancient towns, Berwick is very rich in charities. Apart from the Siamma School, these include £152 yearly paid from the Corporation fund for educational purposes. The sum of £10 is paid annually out of Foreman's bequests for the maintenance of dissenting places of worship. There is another £10 for the maintenance of poor pensioners. About £22

W. Green]     HOLY ISLAND PRIORY, S.W.     [Berwick.

annually has been left for the distribution of bread among the poor; while the sum of £56 16s. per annum is distributed in money from various bequests. There is also £25 annually from Cowle's Charity for the general uses of the poor. It is a pleasure to record that these charities are admirably administered.

Golden Square in Berwick serves to remind the inhabitants of the great importance once enjoyed by their town, for here Edward I. established a mint and assay office, and a large amount of coinage was issued here. Wallace Green is traditionally pointed out as the site of the interment of a portion of the quartered remains of Sir William Wallace, who was executed for high treason in 1305.

There were anciently a large number of religious houses in Berwick, although all trace of most of them has since disappeared. A Benedictine or Cistercian nunnery was founded here by David I. in 1141, and greatly enriched by Edward III. in 1333. The convent was situated about a mile from the town, just off

W. Green]     OLD BELL TOWER.     [Berwick.

the Kelso Road. A monastery of the Franciscans, or Grey Friars was founded at Berwick by Sir John Grey in 1229. The Dominicans, or Black Friars, had a monastery here, founded by Alexander II. of Scotland, in 1230. William the Lion established a house here for the Mathurines, or Trinitarians, between 1142 and 1214. The Carmelites settled here in 1270 under the auspices of Sir John Grey. There was also a hospital called the *Maison Dieu*, at the east end of the town, during the 14th century; and another house dedicated to St. Mary Magdalen, on Magdalen Fields.

As we stated above, Berwick, with many of the towns in Scotland proper, suffered considerably by the union of the two kingdoms. During the 17th and 18th centuries, therefore, it considerably declined. As the frontier town it had up to that time, as we have seen, been the common meeting ground for the high plenipotentiaries of both kingdoms, had been the residence of Kings, and was ever in a state of martial activity. When at last peace was brought about by the union of the two kingdoms it seemed as if the office, or we might almost say the *raison d'etré* of Berwick, had disappeared. Hitherto its occupation had been chiefly one of war; and the town depended largely upon the Garrison, and the train of the high officials who visited the town, for its support. In this respect it was in large measure what may be termed rather an "ornamental" than an industrial town—such a place in fact as St. Andrews was at the same period—and it suffered the same fate as its Scottish compeer, when James VI. of Scotland went south to fill the throne of England. But Berwick has not been content to rest upon its mediæval and feudal reputation, high as that was. Like some warlike old family, finding its former occupation gone in these "piping days of peace," it has cast about for other, and more prosaic, means of making a livelihood, and has, like many of the aforesaid families, in these latter days "taken to trade." At the same

OLD DOORWAY, HOLY ISLAND CHURCH.
*W. Green*]   [*Berwick.*

time it has not allowed the business of life, the smoke of the workshops, and ugly chimney stacks, to destroy its pristine beauty and healthiness. The town derives considerable commercial and industrial importance from the fact of its being the joint terminus of the North Eastern and North British Railways. But it has also considerable industries of its own creation. Chief among these we may reckon that of salmon fishing, which is carried on to a considerable amount in the Tweed. Then there are breweries, agricultural implement manufactories, sail, rope, sack, and manure works, iron foundries and engineering works. The curing of fish also occupies a large section of the community.

Berwick has still another source of prosperity, and that lies in the fact that it is increasing in the regard of tourists. This is as it should be, for few towns in England have so many claims upon the attention of visitors as this old border fortress. The student of history, making this his head-quarters, may visit the scene of all the most famous battles during the sanguinary wars between England and Scotland. Not far away is Homildon Hill and Chevy Chase, the theme of many of our most stirring ballads, while close at hand, too, is the "fatal field of Flodden," so well remembered by the readers of

*W. Green]*    NORHAM CASTLE.    *[Berwick.*

*W. Green]*    GRACE DARLING'S TOMB, BAMBOROUGH.    *[Berwick.*

"Marmion." The antiquary, too, will not find the time hang heavy upon his hands in a town within easy reach of some of the most famous baronial castles of the north—strongholds that have withstood siege after siege. Then, too, there are famous abbeys and churches to attract his attention. Here was the cradle of Christianity in the north; and not far from Berwick is the ancient island of Lindisfarne, celebrated all the world over as the head-quarters of that great missionary bishopric ruled over successively by St. Aidan and St. Cuthbert, the most famous names in the whole of Saxon hagiography. The sportsman will find plenty of opportunities here of exercising his skill, especially if he be a disciple of "Old Isaak," for few British rivers afford such sport as the Tweed, for miles up which there is free rod fishing. The visitor in search of merely health or recreation will find this one of the most bracing towns in the kingdom, while the beauty of its surroundings affords plenty of scope for pleasant excursions.

The people of Berwick have done much to render their ancient town a pleasant resort for visitors. There are a number of excellent hotels, all well conducted, and of moderate tariffs. The retail trades, too, have shown considerable development of late years; and trading establishments may be met here conducted upon principles in every way as enterprising as any to be met in towns of ten times its population. This fact will be clearly demonstrated in the pages which follow.

As an educational centre, too, Berwick possesses many advantages. It has an ancient and amply endowed Grammar School, while its position and healthiness peculiarly befit it to be the site of private schools for both sexes. There are many of these in the town, all well conducted and flourishing.

The modern town of Berwick has in fact risen, Phœnix-like, out of the ruins of the mediæval fortress, and if it has not gained for itself the importance it possessed when it was at once the "key" to Scotland and to England, it has yet attained no small measure of prosperity, and promises in the near future still further development.

As Newcastle has its Tynemouth, and Sunderland its Roker, so has the "good town of Berwick-on-Tweed" a seaside resort for the use and pleasure

W. Green]      TWIZEL BRIDGE AND NORHAM CASTLE.     [Berwick.

of its residents. About one mile east of Tweedmouth, and just south of the headland which bounds Berwick harbour on the south, lies the pleasant seaside villge of Spittal. As the name of the town readily the present century it bore a very bad reputation as a favourite resort of pirates and smugglers, who used to give the Revenue cutters in these parts plenty of work to do. Then a certain romantic interest hung

W. Green]    TWEEDMOUTH, FROM BERWICK QUAY.    [Berwick.

shows us, it was in the Middle Ages the site of a famous religious house or "hospital." Indeed, there seem to have been two such institutions. One called "God's House" was erected before 1327, while, another dedicated to Mary Magdalene, was founded during the 13th century. In later years, however, Spittal entirely lost the air of sanctity which it once wore. For years previous to the commencement of about the little sea-port, but it has long settled down into a prosaic, but at the same time, very pleasant resort, whither the good burgesses of Berwick and Tweedmouth betake themselves to enjoy the sea-bathing

W. Green]    HOLY ISLAND CASTLE.    [Berwick.

and the fresh breezes which sweep across the German Ocean. The people of Spittal, however, are not entirely dependent upon visitors for their subsistence, for the village has a fair amount of trade. This chiefly lies in fish-curing, for which there are several large establishments; while there are also iron, manure and other works. The Berwick and Tweedmouth Gas Company's works are also situated here. It is, however, as a seaside resort that Spittal is best known, and it has certainly many natural advantages to recommend it in this direction. The sands here are smooth and firm, and admirably suited for bathing, while fronting the shore is a fine promenade, always alive with visitors during the season. For those who do not care to trust themselves to the mercies of the sea, excellent sea-water baths are provided, the water being pumped into them by means of a wind-mill. Spittal also possesses a Spa, said to be very beneficial in curing those ills of the flesh for which chalybeates and other tonics are recommended. During the summer season a steam-boat runs between Berwick and Spittal every few minutes, and is always crowded with holiday-makers. Facing the sea are many pretty villa residences, where visitors may take up their quarters. There is a fine church dedicated to St. John the Evangelist, consecrated in 1871. It is of stone in the Early English style, consisting of chancel, nave of three bays and south aisle, and tower. There is also a United Presbyterian church. This church has an interesting origin. It is said that a century and a half ago the south gate of Berwick was kept shut so long on Sabbath mornings, from fear of the Pretender, that the Presbyterians residing in Tweedmouth and Spittal were not able to get into Berwick in time to attend public worship, and divine service was therefore commenced for their convenience in Spittal. During the summer season plenty of amusements are provided here for visitors; and many of the well-to-do people of Berwick and Tweedmouth take up their residence here during these months. The population of the village is very rapidly increasing; and the Corporation of Berwick, who are the lords of the manor and principal landowners, are doing all in their power to make the place one of the pleasantest resorts on the north-east coast.

Among the places we have mentioned as those which should be visited by the tourist making Berwick

W. Green]  BERWICK FROM THE DOCKS.  [Berwick.

his head-quarters, is Holy Island—the cradle of Christianity in Northumbria.

his episcopal see, Aidan founded a monastery, which became the most famous seminary for the preaching

GATEWAY, FORD CASTLE.

Holy Island, or Lindisfarne, as it was then called, first comes into notice in history in 634, when Aidan, a monk of Iona, was sent as a missionary by the Scottish Church to the hitherto almost heathen population of Northumbria. Choosing, probably from the security it offered, this island as the site of

of the Christian faith in the whole of the kingdom. Some idea of the importance of the see may be gathered from the large number of its bishops who were subsequently canonised, the list including such famous names as St. Cuthbert and St. Wilfred. The cathedral built by St. Aidan and enlarged and

W. Green]　　　　FORD CASTLE.　　　　[Berwick.

beautified by subsequent occupants of the see was destroyed by the Danes, when the monks fled with St. Cuthbert's bones, as so delightfully told us by Scott in "Marmion." The Priory Church, the remains of which the visitor will inspect, was built at the close of the 11th century, and was a model on a small scale of Durham cathedral. The church remained perfect till the dissolution of the monasteries, when the buildings were dismantled. The church, which is built of red sandstone, is entered from the west by a doorway ornamented with zig-zag mouldings, under an arcade of five arches. Above this arcade is a round headed window, under a shafted arch, and two square banded towers are attached to the front of the building. The interior is roofless and one side of the nave, with its aisles completely demolished, only the basements of the columns remaining. On the other side stand columns whose shafts resemble those of Durham, their bases and capitals being plain, but these columns are only twelve feet high and five feet in diameter. On the right attached to the Priory are the grey "ruins of the monastery." The extent of these is due to the excavations made in 1888 by Major-General Sir W. Crossman, M.P., with the permission of the Commissioners of Woods and Forests. The castle on Holy Island crowns the entire summit of a curious conical rock of whinstone, called the Beblowe, from whose sides the building seems to spring. It was built about 1500 by Prior Castell, for the defence of the Island. The castle is now used as a station for a detachment of the Coast Brigade of the Royal Artillery, and guns are mounted on the platform at which the volunteers of the island are drilled. The visitor to Holy Island will no doubt bring away with him some of those curious stones found on the sea-shore, known as St. Cuthbert's beads, from the legend which tells us that the ghost of the Saint sits nightly on a neighbouring rock, manufacturing them, using another rock as an anvil. Also, before leaving the neighbourhood of Holy Island the tourist should travel south to Bamborough Castle; and will no doubt rest awhile in the ancient churchyard of the village, where stands the monument of the heroic Grace Darling, whose "musical name is the burden of a beautiful story of that love of man which is the love of Christ translated into human language and deeds."

OLD GATEWAY, HOLY ISLAND PRIORY.
*W. Green]* *[Berwick.*

# GENERAL TRADE

# 1894 - 1994

# 1994

## TINTAGEL HOUSE

### 1894 onwards

1897   James Richardson Black and Co. Ltd - corn, seed and oil cake manufacturers - Love Lane; Works at Spittal.

1911   Company still operating from Love Lane.

1916   Company ceased operating from Love Lane.

1936   September - plans approved for construction of "nine dwelling houses in three flats at Love Lane, Berwick, by Messrs. Gray and Paterson for Mr Albert Williams" - present day Tintagel House. Offices and granaries on right hand side demolished.

Parts of the original building still remain although they are not immediately obvious. For example, the front wall which was part of the entrance into the granary is still evident but has been lowered. In the cobbled courtyard between Tintagel House and the premises now owned by William Cowe and Sons there is a metal boundary mark containing the letters BW to show the extent of Black's and Wilson's (see page 26) properties.

# GENERAL TRADE.

### Messrs. James R. Black and Company, Limited, Manure Manufacturers, Corn, Seed, and Oilcake Merchants. Bone Mill and Manufactory: Spittal. Offices and Granaries: Bridge End.

Mr. J. R. Black.

Mr. R. Thompson
(*Secretary and Manager*).

Messrs. Jas. R. Black and Company's Spittal Works were originally started in 1868, and carried on by the late firm of Crossman and Paulin down to the year 1886, when the present company was formed. As now organised, the Directorate consists of the following gentlemen, all of whom are well known in the commercial circles of the north: — Jas. R. Black, Esq. (Chairman), Jas Dixon, Esq., Thos. Torrance, Esq., John Carr, Esq., C. Hopper, Esq., and G. A. Harrison, Esq. Mr. Ralph Thompson occupies the post of Secretary and Manager. municipal year. Mr. Hopper is Chairman of the Berwick and Tweedmouth Gas Light Company, Limited, and Mr. Carr is a Director of the Berwick Salmon Fisheries Co., Ltd., and Chairman of the Berwick Benefit Building Society. We need scarcely say that under such control the affairs of the parent house above referred to have undergone considerable development. This has been especially the case with respect to manufacturing resources, the Company's Spittal manufactory being now one of the finest in the country, and containing some of the most improved and efficient plant known to the trade. In passing through the works we were particularly struck with the extent and capacity of the bone and phosphate grinding mills, which have been fitted with a variety of costly machinery, and arranged in such a manner as to secure the utmost uniformity and celerity of output. One horizontal steam

Entrance to Offices and Granaries.

It may be mentioned that Mr. Jas. R. Black is a County Alderman of Northumberland, Chairman of the Berwick Union Board of Guardians, Chairman of the Berwick Salmon Fisheries Company, Ltd., and Director of the Constantine Phosphate Company, Algeria, whilst Mr. G. A. Harrison is a Town Councillor of Berwick, and serves the borough in the capacity of Sheriff during the present engine and one vertical steam engine of the latest type, and together developing about 150 h.-p., are used for driving purposes, and it is not too much to observe that taken all round the appliances and accommodation at disposal are of a character which fully justifies the firm's prestige. Supplementing the departments noted, we find extensive dissolving chambers, where the powdered

FOURTH FLOOR GRANARY, LOVE LANE.

phosphates are converted into superphosphates by the action of sulphuric acid. The Company's offices and sample rooms are situated in Love Lane, Bridge End, Berwick, and adjoining them they have enormous granaries, seed stores, and stores for oil cakes and other cattle feeding stuffs, the latter containing an excellent plant of machinery for breaking cake and grinding and preparing cattle foods generally. As affording some idea of the magnitude of these premises, we may state that they occupy three sides of a spacious square, each structure being several stories in height. Upwards of sixty hands are employed at the Spittal Works alone, whilst a large staff of porters and clerks has to be maintained at the granaries and offices. The superior characteristics of Messrs. Black and Company's staple products are too widely known to require recapitulation. We give below, however, the full text of an Analytical report the firm recently received from Dr. Augustus Voelcker and Sons, the eminent agricultural specialists:—

Analytical Laboratory, 22, Tudor Street, New Bridge Street, London, E.C.
Result of Analysis of a Sample of Vitriolated Bones sent by Messrs. Jas. R. Black and Company, Limited.
Sealed, "Jas. R. Black and Company."

| | |
|---|---|
| Moisture ... ... | 13·08 |
| Organic Matter and Water of Combination ... ... ... | 26·00 |
| Monobasic Phosphate of Lime ... ... | 9·95 |
| (Equal to Tribasic Phosphate of Lime rendered Soluble by Acid... ... ... | 15·59) |
| Insoluble Phosphates | 26·29 |
| Sulphate of Lime, &c. | 23·15 |
| Insoluble Siliceous Matter ... ... | 1·53 |
| | 100·00 |
| Containing Nitrogen ... | 3·13 |
| Equal to Ammonia ... | 3·80 |

(Signed)
AUGUSTUS VOELCKER & SONS.

As regards alike artificial manures and grain and farm seeds, Messrs. Black and Company are undoubtedly doing an extensive and steadily expanding trade, not only locally but throughout the north. All manures sent out by them are guaranteed up to standard analyses which are clearly set forward in the firm's annual circular, and which exhibit high fertilising percentages of soluble phosphates and

FIFTH FLOOR GRANARY, LOVE LANE.

# 1994

## TINTAGEL HOUSE

The "Cat Wall", at the back of the original property.

# 1994

## B & M MOTORS

### 1894 onwards

1897    James Richardson Black and Co. Limited - corn seed and oil cake merchants and manure manufacturers - works a North Greenwich Road, Spittal.

1911    James Richardson Black still operating there.

1925    Company has ceased trading.

1948    Fisons Limited - fertiliser manufacturers and agricultural feeding stuff merchants.

1973    Peter Spellman Limited - car storage

1985    B & M Motors - car repairers

Although it is not been possible to pinpoint the actual building used by James R. Black and Company in Spittal, it may have been these premises.

Alan Batey and George Mark, the owners of B & M Motors, have operated their motor vehicle repair business from these premises for the past 10 years. They employ one mechanic and repair all makes of cars from Fiats to Audis.

### Opening Hours
Monday - Friday :    8.30 am to 5.30 pm
Saturday:            9.30 am to 1.00 pm

### Charge/Goods Sold
Labour Charge :    £11.00 per hour

nitrogen. Special manures are made up to suit customers' individual requirements, the guarantees in all cases being stated on the invoice. The comprehensive standard qualities kept in stock, however, are fully capable of meeting average agrarian exigencies, and we can confidently recommend them to the attention of all and sundry who are anxious to secure a reliable and, at the same time, distinctly economical fertiliser for any kind of crop or soil. As a proof of the energetic manner in which the firm look after the interests of the community they serve, we may mention that while particulars for this article were being obtained Messrs. Black and Co. were receiving their first consignment of Algerian Phosphate per S.S. "Nicosian," this being the first shipment to Great Britain from the Constantine Mine. This Phosphate is destined to play an important part in the fertiliser trade and the discovery comes at an opportune moment, when the supply of a cheap and reliable superphosphate to the British farmer is a consummation devoutly to be wished. It speaks no little for the probity and straightforwardness which have hitherto characterised Messrs. Black's methods of doing business, to find that the "Fertilisers and Feeding Stuffs Act," which came into operation on the 1st of January last, has not necessitated any appreciable changes in their system of dealing. They have always made it a practice to guarantee manures and to give them a correct title and description, which is practically all that the Act requires, whilst with respect to feeding stuffs they have only to adhere to their usual principle of either guaranteeing purity, or plainly stating that the cakes are compounded, to keep well within the limits of legislative restrictions on the subject. By way of conclusion we may mention that Messrs. J. R. Black and Company's representatives attend all the principal markets within a fifty mile radius of Berwick, and price lists, circulars, analyses, &c., may always be obtained on application either at the market stands or the Company's offices.

SPITTAL WORKS FROM THE ENTRANCE.

MILL IN SPITTAL WORKS.

## The Border Brewery Company, Brewers, Maltsters, Wine & Spirit Merchants, Aerated Water Manufacturers.
### Offices: Silver Street.

Mr. Henning (*Managing Partner*).

The Border Brewery, famous for its fine ales, has naturally a right to prominent notice in our present work. It is not only of interest as an important centre of industry, the seat of production of some of the finest beverages in the Border counties, but it is also of interest from a historic point of view. It was founded in the last century, and has during the whole of its existence formed a chief feature in the resources of the town. Its history may, in fact, be considered an important part of the history of Berwick itself during that period. The purest quality. This water is drawn from mineral springs, and is considered by experts to be one of the finest waters in the Kingdom both for brewing and for aerated water manufacturing. The brewery is fitted with a twenty-five quarter plant of the most improved modern character, securing efficiency and economy in the working, and the malt mills, mash tuns, coppers, coolers, refrigerators, and fermenting vessels are models of construction and equipment. From the malt going into the copper until the beer is drawn off in the racking cellars, every operation is conducted with scientific care and judgment, and the most scrupulous cleanliness is maintained throughout in every detail. Only the choicest hops are used, and the malt is of the finest quality, made by the firm themselves from the best barleys procurable in the Berwick district. With high class malt and hops, and water of rare excellence, and highly trained ability in supervision, it is no wonder that the India pale ales and XXX stout produced by the Border Brewery have gained a wide-spread celebrity both in England and Scotland, the increase in the quantity of stout brewed being especially marked. The maltings here have a frontage to the main street, and are well constructed

The Border Brewery.

business, however, is now developing at a more rapid rate than ever it did before, since Mr. Henning assumed the practical management in 1887. Up to that date it was owned by Mr. Robert Douglas, who carried it on with enterprise, but the change from a single individual to a private Company has proved a turning point in its career by bringing in fresh capital and energy, and especially in securing the advantage of Mr. Henning's acknowledged ability and practical experience as managing partner. The offices are situated in Silver Street, and comprise a handsome suite of public and private chambers, well appointed throughout; and close by are sample-rooms, beer stores, wine vaults, and spirit stores, besides extensive maltings. Leaving these for the moment, let us have a glance at the brewery and mineral water factory, situated together near the Dock at Tweedmouth. These works have one great advantage, viz., the unrivalled water supply, which is abundant and of the with modern steeps, germinating floors, and improved kilns, and the output is large. The mineral water works are in the same group of buildings, and have a very complete plant, capable of turning out all varieties of mineral and aerated waters. Here, again, of course, the water supply is of vital importance, and the improved character of the plant obviates any possible risk of metallic or other contamination. Only the purest syrups, essences, and other ingredients are used, and we have seen few manufactories of this kind in which such a degree of cleanliness was maintained. The bottle-washing, bottling, gas-generating, aerating, and labelling arrangements are faultless, and the various operations are got through with a smoothness and rapidity, and with such dainty cleanliness, that speaks volumes for the perfect organisation and supervision of the works. Lemonade, ginger-beer, potass, soda, lithia, and seltzer waters, champagne cider, &c., are turned out, as well as the noted speciality of the firm, their delicious "Phiz."

# 1994

## CRAWFORDS JOINERY
## THE BORDER BREWERY COMPANY

### 1894 onwards

1910    Border Brewery Limited - brewery

1926    Border Brewery Company merged with brewers Johnson and Darling

1934    Brewery purchased by Vaux and Associated Breweries Limited

1937    Brewery ceased operating

1980    Premises purchased by Alan and Carol Crawford for use as a joinery factory

1992    Border Brewery Company Limited formed. Beer is again brewed on the premises.

1994    Border Brewery Company Limited sold to Andrew Burrows and Leslie Orde.

Crawford's Joinery, owned by Alan Crawford has operated from these premises for the past 14 years. The company makes a wide range of windows and doors and employs ten full time and one part time member of staff.

### Opening Hours

Monday :     8.00 am to 5.00 pm
Tuesday - Thursday :     8.00 am to 8.00 pm
Friday :     8.00 am to 4.00 pm
Saturday :     8.00 am to noon

### THE BORDER BREWERY COMPANY

In 1992 Alan Crawford formed the Border Brewery Company Limited and started brewing beer on the site again after a break of over 50 years. In June 1994 the brewery was taken over by Andrew Burrows and Leslie Orde who now run the company with the help of Mark Satchwell, their sales manager. The brewery leases part of the building from Crawfords Joinery and makes six types of beer including Rudolf's Ruin and SOB. Up to 500 bottles and 10 - 12 barrels of beer are produced each week.

As far as possible, the firm use local ingredients for its beer, including water from St Cuthbert's Well - which is on the premises - and malt from Simpsons Malt in Tweedmouth. The beer is sold throughout the country.

# 1994

## BLACKBURN AND PRICE LIMITED

### 1894 onwards

1910    Border Brewery Limited - brewers and mineral water manufacturers - 12 Silver Street

1926    Border Brewery Company merged with Johnson and Darling Limited., brewers. Company renamed Berwick Breweries Limited.

1934    Company bought by Vaux and Associated Breweries Limited but retained its name

1936    The Berwick Breweries Limited - wholesale and retail at 12 Silver Street

1948    Premises purchased by Blackburn and Price Limited

The firm of Blackburn and Price was established in 1946 by William Blackburn and Jack Price. Originally it operated from premises behind the Governor's House in Palace Green but in the late 1940s it took over the burnt out malting and grain warehouses of the former Border Brewery in Silver Street. The company still operate from these premises and have built up a thriving business selling and servicing cars. At present the company employs 21 full time and one part time member of staff in various capacities from motor mechanics to car salesmen and administrative staff. They sell a wide range of new Vauxhall cars including Cavaliers and Corsas as well as all makes of second hand cars. The present Managing Director is Peter Dixon.

### Opening Hours
Monday - Friday :    8.00 am to 5.00 pm
Saturday:    8.00 am to 4.00 pm

### Charges/Goods Sold
New Cars:    £7,200 to £27,000
Used Cars:    £1,500 to £15,000
Parts:    20 pence to £2,000
Vehicle Servicing:    £35 upwards

The plant in these works is McEwen's patent, erected by Dan Rylands, and driven by steam power. Both the mineral water factory and the brewery are lighted by electricity, the installation being a highly efficient one, the brewery having eighty fine lights of 16-candle power each. The buildings here form a square, with cooperage, cask-washing and other subsidiary departments in the yard, and the compact arrangement, the extensive use of labour-saving appliances, and the exceptional facilities for cheap transport both by rail and water, tend powerfully to reduce the cost of production, and account to a great extent for the very moderate quotations at which the firm are able to offer their productions. Returning to Silver Street, we find here extensive maltings turning out great quantities of high class malt, and fitted with screening appliances, &c. Close by are immense stone-vaulted beer cellars, said to be the finest of their kind in the North. They contain enormous stocks of the Border Brewery's ales and stouts, besides ales and stouts by Bass, Guinness, and other eminent firms. The Company do a large bottling trade, for which they have

THE BORDER BREWERY—STORES AND CELLARS.

THE BORDER BREWERY—MINERAL WATER WORKS.

very complete arrangements. The wine cellars are extensive and contain large stocks of choice old vintage wines, champagnes, clarets, ports, sherries, Moselle, Burgundy, &c., and here also they have bottling facilities. The firm have a very extensive connection in wines and spirits all over the counties on both sides of the Border, Mr. Henning's wide experience and knowledge of wines giving him great advantages in this respect, while he also makes the most of the facilities the large amount of cellarage at hand affords keeping the bins filled with some of the rarest vintages of ports, sherries, and sparkling wines that can be bought. The Company have a private bond at the quay, with all facilities for vatting, which is filled with whiskies, rums, and brandies for their general trade. A very extensive trade is done, whiskies, wines, ales and stout being sent to Newcastle, Manchester, Glasgow, and other distant centres. The partners are well known and highly respected in the Berwick district, Mr. Douglas being Town Clerk of Berwick, and Mr. Henning a gentleman of high standing in commercial circles.

## Mr. George Black, Boiler Builder, Tweedmouth Boiler Works.

The Tweedmouth boiler works probably constitute the oldest boiler-making establishment in the North, having been started so far back as the year 1790 by the grandfather of the present proprietor. From comparatively modest beginnings the works have risen to a position of considerable importance, the existing premises being much more commodious than those originally occupied, and the trade extending over a much wider area. Every practical man will admit that mild steel boilers possess marked advantages over any form of iron boiler hitherto reproduce them for the benefit of our readers. In the first place, it was claimed that thickness for thickness, mild steel boilers were distinctly stronger than their iron prototypes. Secondly, that the texture of steel being closer than that of iron, boilers made from the former material exhibited little or no tendency to blister, and were capable of withstanding the pitting action of bad water and the consequent grooving at the seams, much more effectively than boilers made from iron. Thirdly, that plate manufacturers could supply larger plates of steel than of iron, without extra cost. For example the flue or tube of an iron boiler was usually made in six plates, whilst by adopting steel Mr. Black made two plates suffice—this, of course, meaning a great saving to the customer. After some years' experience on different classes of steel-made boilers, Mr. Black determined to lay down special plant for their manufacture, and if possible to improve the design and augment the efficiency of the work produced. That he has been entirely successful in these latter regards is amply indicated by the demand which exists for the various types of boilers now turned

Exterior of Tweedmouth Boiler Works.

produced. Mr. George Black was one of the first to recognise these advantages and some years ago issued a circular succinctly setting them forth. As time and experience have fully justified the statements referred to, we may briefly out, as well as by the large number of orders received from the principal engineering firms of the Tyne and other centres. As a matter of fact, the boilers produced at Mr. Black's works have fewer seams and fewer rivets than many others

# 1 9 9 4

## DRUMMOND'S YARD

### 1894 onwards

1897    George Black - boiler, iron tank and cistern and boiler covering manufacturer - Tweedmouth Boiler Works.

1906    George Black and Sons - boiler, iron tank, cistern and marine boiler manufacturers and creosote plant manufacturers for estate work.

1925    George Black and Sons Limited - boiler makers

1929    Application by Mr A. Weir to build houses on site of former Boiler Works.

The buildings used by George Black on land adjoining the railway embankment behind Main Street in Tweedmouth have been demolished. The area is now used as a Travelling People's Caravan Site operated by David Drummond.

**KELLY'S DIRECTORY, 1906**

# The Alnwick Guardian & County Advertiser.

### A SPLENDID ADVERTISING MEDIUM

From Tyne to Tweed, from Cheviot to the German Ocean, circulating in the homes of country gentlemen, town residents, the miners of the great colliery districts, the agriculturists of the county, and the fishermen of the seaboard.

Patronized by the principal advertisers, including the County and Local Authorities, Auctioneers, Land Agents, &c.

#### CHEAP RATES FOR CONTINUED ADVERTISEMENTS.

FRIDAY, FOR SATURDAY.  + + +  56 COLUMNS.  1d.

### Publisher: JAMES C. GRANT,

Publishing Offices: Bondgate Within & Market Street, Alnwick; & at Amble.

Nat Tel. 034. Telegrams: "GUARDIAN, ALNWICK."

---

Telegraphic Address: "BOILERS, BERWICK." Telephone No. 7.

# BLACK'S CREOSOTING PLANT,

CONSISTING OF

### Pressure Cylinder, Oil Tank and Set of Self-Contained Pumps.

The accompanying illustration is the most suitable and up-to-date method of Creosoting Timber Rails, Gate Posts, &c., to meet the requirements of Landowners, to suit small and large Estates.

**SITES INSPECTED AND ESTIMATES GIVEN.**

Suitable Oil for Creosoting supplied.

### ESTABLISHED 1790.

**GEORGE BLACK & SONS,** Tweedmouth Boiler Works, **BERWICK-ON-TWEED,**

Makers of Lancashire, Cornish, Multitubular, Vertical & Locotype Boilers for Land & Marine Purposes.

---

# The Birtley Iron Company and Owners of Pelaw Main Collieries,

## BIRTLEY, COUNTY OF DURHAM.

MANUFACTURERS OF EVERY DESCRIPTION OF

## ENGINES, CASTINGS, FORGINGS and MACHINERY

For Land, Marine and Colliery Purposes, Iron and Steel Works, &c., Gas and Water Works, Bridges, Boilers, &c.  SPECIALITIES—Rolling Mills and Pumping Sets.

### London Office:—46, CANNON ST., E.C.

P.O. Telephone No. 379. Nat. Telephone No. 2 Birtley. Telegraphic Address: "BIRTLEY, NEWCASTLE."

---

*The Genuine Local Newspaper.* Established **1854**.

**A SUCCESSFUL NEWSPAPER ENSURES .. SUCCESSFUL RESULTS TO ADVERTISERS.**

ADVERTISE in the

# AUCKLAND TIMES

—— And your Business will Increase.

SEND A POSTCARD FOR ADVERTISEMENT RATES.

Proprietors: **THE AUCKLAND TIMES AND HERALD LTD.,**
Printers, Stationers and Publishers. *Registered Offices:*
*(Manager, J. D. ATHEY).* 2, SOUTH ROAD, BISHOP AUCKLAND.

D. N. & C. W.

extant, thus reducing the wearing action of both fire and water on the boiler seams, which, as everybody knows, are the weakest parts. The premises in which the manufacture is carried on, are situated in Main Road, Tweedmouth, close to the foot of the railway embankment. They comprise spacious erecting, rivetting and plate sheds, equipped with powerful overhead cranes and improved cutting, punching and rolling machinery, capable of dealing with steel plates up to 1¼in. thickness. There is a commodious flanging department with the full complement of fires, together with rivet makers' and blacksmiths' shops and other conveniences, whilst in view of possible structural extensions additional ground has been acquired, which brings the total area of the property up to about two acres. Mr. Black turns out Lancashire, Cornish, multitubular, vertical and locomills, orders in this connection having been received from many of the leading paper-making firms in Kent, Oxford, Manchester, Aberdeen, Glasgow and Edinburgh. Wrought iron tanks and cisterns, wrought iron cylinders for land rollers, rivetted kitchen range boilers, saddle boilers for green-houses, case-hardened bone mill cutter plates, gas-holders and the like also constitute items of the output. Considerable attention is devoted to the construction of boilers adapted for farmers and others using small power, the specialities put forward in this line being exceptionally strong, cheap, safe and lasting. Standard sizes from four horse-power to eight horse-power are generally kept in stock, and all necessary mountings and fittings supplied and fixed if required. Boilers are repaired and altered, examined, reported upon, or tested at the shortest notice

INTERIOR OF TWEEDMOUTH BOILER WORKS.

type steel boilers suitable for land and marine purposes alike. He commenced making marine multitubular boilers a few years ago, each example being constructed to Lloyd's requirements and passed by the surveyor of that body before leaving the works. The all-round satisfaction given by this class of boiler is perhaps best illustrated by the circumstance that over twenty-two of them have been supplied to one firm in Newcastle during the past three or four years. Various types of boilers have also been sent to such distant parts of the globe as China, Japan, and Australia, and it may be mentioned that material and mountings with plans and templates for erection at destination, can be shipped when required. A further speciality of the house is the manufacture of roasting pans for paper and on the most reasonable terms, and although Mr. Black does not term himself an engineer, nor make engines, at times he purchases an engine and fits it up complete with boiler and mountings suitable for farm purposes. Second-hand portable engines, which have been repaired and put into working order for driving thrashing machines, etc., are consequently often on hand at the works. Taken as a whole the concern may be fairly described as by far the largest and most notable steel and iron boiler-making enterprise in this part of the country. The proprietor is not only well known in trade circles, but interests himself also in the welfare of the locality, being a Guardian of the Poor, and President of the Tweedmouth Reading Room.

## Messrs. Paxton and Purves, Plain and Fancy Drapers, Hosiers, Silk Mercers, etc., Ladies' and Gentlemen's Outfitters, Scotsgate House, High Street.

Scotsgate House, formerly the residence of a mayor of Berwick, has during the last few years been turned to practical account by Messrs. Paxton and Purves as a first-class modern drapery and outfitting establishment. The site of the premises in High Street, close to Scotsgate, and easily accessible from all sides, is one of the most favourable in the town, and no trouble or expense has been spared to thoroughly remodel the premises themselves so as to adapt them to the requirements of a high-class modern business. The business of the firm is a very old established one, dating from the year 1802, when it was founded by the late Mr. John Paxton. The premises occupied were then in Western Lane, as is authoritatively declared by a quaint and circumstantial old document now framed in the office of the firm. Afterwards the business has changed much since the beginning of the century, and even during recent years it has undergone a complete revolution. However, the business of this firm has always occupied a unique and leading position, and as it was judiciously adapted to the progressive requirements of the times, new departments were added from time to time, until the business became a very large and comprehensive one, including every branch of ladies' and gentlemen's outfitting. It is at present reckoned the finest retail establishment of its kind between Newcastle and Edinburgh, and has a large and influential patronage from the leading town and county families within a radius of many miles around Berwick. The building has a fine frontage of 60 feet in length, with an imposing double front of plate glass in High Street. The exceptional facilities for displaying specialities, new fashions, &c., are fully availed of, and the show-windows of Scotsgate House form a constant attraction to passers by. In the centre is a handsome vestibule entrance adorned with a beautiful

SCOTSGATE HOUSE.

was removed successively to the corner of Hide Hill and High Street, and to 53, High Street, and finally, about six years ago, to the present premises. They say "a rolling stone gathers no moss," but it was not moss the proprietors of the business wanted to gather, and in any case their several removals were but results of their progressive development and prosperity, as the cause in each case was that the business had outgrown the available accommodation. From the beginning the business has remained in the same family, so that the accumulated experience of over ninety years, and all the personal and family pride in advancing the prestige of the house, have been important factors in maintaining its reputation as a first class town and country trade. The founder was succeeded by his two sons, Messrs. E. and W. Paxton, who carried on the business in partnership until Mr. E. Paxton's death in 1872. The surviving partner, Mr. W. Paxton, and present head of the firm, then admitted into partnership his nephew, Mr. Thomas Purves, these two gentlemen now constituting the firm. The drapery trade fanlight of stained glass, and from this vestibule doors lead off to the right and left to the separate shops, that on the left being devoted to general and fancy drapery, and that on the right to gentlemen's bespoke tailoring, ready-made outfitting, hosiery, gloves, &c. To the rear are large tailoring-rooms, cutting and fitting-rooms, &c. The splendidly decorated show-rooms for mantles and millinery, &c., are on the first floor, and are appointed throughout in good taste, comparing well with any similar show-rooms in Scotland. Private fitting-rooms for ladies, and private show-rooms for baby linen and ladies' underclothing are also provided, and a full staff of milliners and dressmakers are employed on the premises, so that wedding trousseaux, travelling outfits, costumes, mourning outfits, &c., are turned out in the very best style, perfect in fit and finish. The display of fashionable dress fabrics is thoroughly representative of the very latest fashions, and in French and British millinery, hat and bonnet shapes, flowers, feathers, &c., the stock is one of the best we have seen anywhere in the provinces. The firm have

# 1994

## PAXTON AND PURVES LIMITED

### 1894 onwards

1897    Paxton and Purves - general drapers and tailors

1929    Paxton and Purves - drapers

1953    Paxton and Purves Limited - drapers

1983    Paxton and Purves Limited - drapers (member of Associated Independent Stores )

1985    Purchased by Wilson Distributors (Scotland ) Limited

Paxton and Purves, an old established department store in Berwick is now owned by Wilson Distributors but was originally a family business run by the Paxton and Purves families. The business has operated from these premises in Marygate since 1888 and was incorporated as a Limited Company in 1908. Mr Tom Purves, the last surviving member of the family and former Chairman of the Company, died in 1992.

Today Paxton and Purves still sell a wide range of ladies' and mens' wear and furniture. However, unlike 1894, they now only employ three full time and five part time members of staff.

Part of the original building is now occupied by the Berwick Bus Shop.

# 1994

## PAXTON AND PURVES LIMITED

**Opening Hours**
Monday - Saturday: 9.30 am to 5.30 pm

**Goods Sold**
Skirts: £21.99 upwards
Jackets: £29.99 to £99.99
Blouses: £25.00 upwards
Dining Table and 4 Chairs: £499.00
Glass Top Lamp Table: £115.00

arrangements that ensure their being constantly supplied with the latest fashions and novelties in each department, and all their goods are obtained direct from the most reliable houses in the trade, no inferior goods being stocked in any department. In gentlemen's tailoring the firm have a special reputation for evening dress, business and professional suits, riding and hunting outfits, &c., and a first-class cutter is employed, so that none but thoroughly high-class work is sent out. Owing, however, to the great resources of the firm, their exceptional experience of the different branches of the trade, and their well organised system of business, their prices compare well with those of any similar house, either in London or the provinces. Mention must also be made of the carpet department, this being a great speciality with the firm. Entirely separate accommodation is set apart for these goods, and abundant room for choice will be found in the large stock of Brussels carpets, Kensington art squares, Istakhr, Kashyar, and other English and foreign makes. The department also embraces floor cloths, linoleums, curtains, etc., etc. The premises, of which we have given but a very imperfect sketch, extend back from High Street a distance of 150 feet, and, with gardens, &c., extend right back to Bank Hill. Messrs. Paxton and Purves employ a staff of about 60 hands, and every facility is provided for the prompt and careful execution of orders. Altogether the business is conducted on the most advanced lines of modern enterprise, and the connection is steadily increasing.

DRAPERY DEPARTMENT.

MILLINERY DEPARTMENT.

## Messrs. John Wilson and Son, Ironmongers, Plumbers, Gasfitters, Bellhangers, Glaziers, etc., and General Hardware Merchants, Wholesale & Retail Glass Warehouse, Victoria Buildings, Bridge End.

MR. J. WILSON.

This business, as will be gathered from its descriptive title, is of a very comprehensive character, and it is, moreover, a very old-established concern, having been founded over 100 years ago, and a brief sketch of its history and operations will, we think, prove extremely interesting. The late Mr. John Wilson succeeded to it forty years ago, and carried it on until 1884, when it was continued under the style of John Wilson and Son, Mr. John Wilson, junior, being the sole proprietor. The original premises were at 41, Bridge Street, and the business was transferred to the present address in 1887, the shop having this especially applying to the cooking and heating apparatus, which are of the newest kinds, and constructed according to proved economical principles. The general stock embraces a wide variety of goods, and includes cabinet-maker's ironmongery, engineers' tools, gas and steam tubing, hot water pipe and fittings, gaseliers and brackets, ship, boat and house lamps in great variety, scales and weights, electro-plated wares, watches, barometers, bronzes, marble clocks, churns and dairy utensils, domestic washing machines, wringers and mangles, rubber goods, garden and agricultural tools and implements, basinettes and mail carts, bent glass shades, china, glass and earthenware, brushes, turnery goods, tin, iron, and enamelled hollow ware, and many other goods too numerous to mention. Iron and brass bedsteads of new design and well finished are on hand, also hair and wool mattresses and straw palliasses, chair beds and cushions. A stock is also held of Rogers and Sons', and Needham, Veal and Tyzack's celebrated Sheffield table and pocket cutlery. Mr. Wilson is also an extensive importer of and dealer in Belgian sheet glass, British plate, stained window glass, etc., etc.; he also makes a speciality of imperishable memorial wreaths, of which he has the largest show between Newcastle and Edinburgh. A large staff of efficient and experienced workmen are employed in executing all sorts of work

VICTORIA BUILDINGS.

been constructed out of what was originally a dwelling-house, and named "Victoria Buildings" by Mr. John Wilson, junior, himself. The premises comprise a conspicuous corner shop facing old Berwick Bridge, with tastefully dressed windows in both Bridge End and West Street; there are also extensive warehouses where reserve stocks are kept, as well as admirably equipped workshops in the rear. As a plumber and gasfitter, etc., Mr. Wilson has a wide-spread reputation and the work executed by him is its own guarantee. A large selection of sanitary appliances, etc., connected with the trade is held in stock so that customers are attended to with promptness and despatch. In the builder's ironmongery department there is a good stock of register grates, open and close fire ranges, register tiled grates, tiled hearths, nails, screws, mason's and carpenter's tools, representing the latest ideas in invention and manufacture, connected with stove and range fitting, plumbing, gas-fitting, bell-hanging, glazing, sanitary and hot water engineering, and every description of repairs are also carried out. The proprietor is agent for the Plate Glass Insurance Company and the North British and Mercantile Fire and Life Insurance Company. Mr. Wilson is an enterprising and genial, as well as a thoroughly practical man, and gives a constant personal attention to every branch of the business, so that customers can rely on their orders being performed in a manner at once satisfactory to all concerned. As we stated at the commencement, the concern has been established over 100 years, but the large and valuable connection Mr. Wilson has gained, and the great confidence he enjoys, has been founded not so much on his long standing, as on the thoroughly reliable and satisfactory nature of all goods supplied, and work done by him.

# 1994

## WILLIAM COWE AND SONS

### 1894 onwards

1897    John Wilson and Son - plumber and ironmongers.

1910    George Martin - stationer, printer and publisher of the Berwick Mercury, Times and Warder.

1955    Martin, the printers moved to premises in Spittal

1959    McNeil Brothers - Pianos, Radios

1961    West Cumberland Farmers

1964    William Cowe and Sons - confectioners. Wholesale Department

The firm of William Cowe and Sons, makers of the famous Berwick Cockles, is said to have been established in 1801. The business started in Marygate and then for many years operated solely from Nos. 64 - 66 Bridge Street, now their grocery department. In the 1960s this family business expanded and they opened a wholesale department in Victoria Buildings which they had owned since the early 1900s but had leased in the interim. Today William Cowe and Sons employs six full time and two part time staff and sells confectionery and other goods to various businesses and clubs throughout North Northumberland and the Borders.

### Opening Hours
Monday - Saturday :    9.00 am to 5.00 pm

# 1994

## KINGS ARMS HOTEL

### 1894 onwards

1897    Family and Commercial Hotel, job and post horses, carriages gigs, etc. - Proprietor : John Carr

1902    Proprietor : Mrs John Carr

1910    Family and Commercial Hotel, job master and motor garage. Proprietor : Hugo Reinecke

1925    "Entirely refurbished and redecorated". Proprietor : Charles Wilson

1938    Proprietor : Mrs Charles Wilson

1952    Proprietor : H.H.Hessling

1962    Proprietor : Golden Star Hotels (Northern Limited)

1973    Proprietor : Clydesdale and Commonwealth Hotels Limited

The Kings Arms Hotel, a former coaching inn, established in Hide Hill several centuries ago, is now owned by Gatehouse Hotels Limited. Although part of the building used in 1894 is now occupied by the Trustees Savings Bank, the hotel has expanded up Hide Hill into the premises formerly occupied by W.A.Logan ( see page 27 ). Today the Kings Arms is still a busy hotel providing accommodation for visitors from all over the world, as well as a venue for conferences, banquets and local functions. Its facilities include 36 guest bedrooms; The Kings Room restaurant; The Royal Suite for banquets and conferences; the Garden Terrace Restaurant; Cafe Pizzaz; and the Assembly Rooms in which Charles Dickens gave readings from his works in 1858 and 1861.The hotel employs twenty nine full time and four part time staff and is open 24 hours every day of the year.

**Prices**
Single Room :                              £46 .50 per night
Double Room :                              £59 .50 per night
3 Course Table D'Hote Dinner with Coffee : £15 .00

## Mr. Joseph Weatherston,
### Slater, Plasterer, Builder, etc., High Street.

The above concern was established upwards of a century ago, and has always been conducted in the name of Joseph Weatherston, the present principal having succeeded his uncle—also named Joseph Weatherston—on the decease of the latter in 1870. Throughout the county and neighbouring districts the enterprise has been continuously associated with the best aspects of the building and allied trades, and its present position is one of distinct prominence and well recognised influence. In fact, it is not too much to say that for years past, and especially recently, the house has invariably had to do with the principal building, contracting, and other works carried out in the neighbourhood —a circumstance alone sufficient to indicate the soundness of its organisation and the amplitude of its resources. Mr. Weatherston's head-quarters are situated in High Street, Berwick, in close proximity to Scot Gate, and immediately adjoining the town walls. The premises consist of a spacious yard, 200 feet by 100 feet, access to which is obtained through a suitable gateway, on the left of which are the general office and the private office of the principal. A commodious range of stores is likewise available, and here in the yard we find comprehensive stocks of building materials of every description, together with an exceptionally large supply of the usual accessories and appurtenances of the trade. Although, as our readers will no doubt be aware, Mr. Weatherston devotes by far the major portion of his time and energies to public affairs, he still continues to exercise a controlling influence over the transactions of the concern, and as he is assisted by a capable manager, matters steadily continue to progress on the old lines of efficiency and stability. Both as a man of business and as a public servant, Mr. Weatherston has long enjoyed the unqualified respect and esteem of his fellow townsmen. His work in connection with various movements for the improvement of Berwick and the benefit of her residents will always redound to his credit, and his services in the Borough Council Chamber were fittingly recognised in November last by his election to the Mayoral Chair of the Municipality, the duties of which important office he has so far fulfilled with remarkable tact and capability. He is well known as a liberal supporter of every movement calculated to result in the enhanced well being of the neighbourhood, whilst as a worker in the cause of progress his zeal apparently knows no end.

## The King's Arms Hotel, Family and Commercial, Hide Hill, Berwick-upon-Tweed.
### Proprietor - - Mr. John Carr.

A good hotel is at one and the same time an indication of prosperity in any town, and also to a large extent the cause of prosperity. Travellers, whether on business or pleasure will be sure to give any town a "wide berth" if they know they will have a difficulty in obtaining comfortable hotel accommodation at moderate rates, and on the other hand it is surprising what slight pretexts are sufficient to attract visitors, when they know that they have excellent hotels before them. The King's Arms Hotel, Berwick, has for many generations enjoyed a wide-spread celebrity. In the old coaching days it was a noted hostelry, and since then it has maintained its reputation, and is acknowledged by all visitors to be one of the most comfortable hotels in the Border counties. Owing to its great popularity it has attracted large numbers of visitors, and, with the extension of railways and the general improvement in locomotion, the demands on its accommodation became so great that the proprietor, Mr. John Carr, has been obliged to extend it on both sides, taking in the adjoining buildings. This makes it look almost like three hotels in one, but although the external appearance is somewhat wanting in compactness, it is at the same time a very handsome edifice,

THE KING'S ARMS HOTEL.

forming one of the principal architectural features of modern Berwick. The hotel stands in a convenient and accessible position amid pleasant surroundings. The interior is very handsomely appointed, and contains, in addition to coffee, dining, commercial, smoking, and other public rooms, a number of well furnished private suites, and also a large well appointed billiard-room. There are about thirty bed-rooms, all airy, cheerful, and well appointed, and kept scrupulously clean. There are also bath-rooms, lavatories, etc., and in fact every comfort of a home with all the conveniences of a first class modern hotel. The cooking and catering are faultless, the attendance prompt and civil, and the charges throughout are strictly moderate. Mr. Carr personally superintends the whole management, and spares no pains to ensure the comfort of his guests. The cellar contains an ample stock of rare old vintage wines, choice blends of whiskey and brandy, etc., and none but the highest class of beverages are supplied. In connection with the hotel there is a capital posting establishment, which is a great convenience for visiting the many places of interest in this district.

## Mr. John Wilson, Monumental Sculptor and Marble Mason, Bridge End, Tweedmouth.

Mr. John Wilson's premises at Bridge End, Tweedmouth, constitute quite a noteworthy feature of the resources of the district, inasmuch as they not only form the head-quarters of an especially old established business, but they have further been arranged and laid out, as it were, on a principle that is quite as novel as it is attractive. The trade display made by the average monumental sculptor cannot be regarded as in any sense inspiring. Too often it resolves itself into an altogether unconsidered jumble of tablets, head-stones, and monuments, pedestalled on bricks, and propped up by sundry loose pieces of wood. Mr. Wilson has gone one better in this connection than the general run of his fellow craftsmen, however, by substituting for the usual unsightly yard a trim ornamental garden, where the productions of his chisel can be exhibited with becoming and reasonable advantage. The statuary, fountain work, busts, etc., here to be seen, certainly reflect the highest credit on the artistic capacity of their originator, and when we come to inspect the space set

MONUMENTAL WORKS, BRIDGE END.

apart for the display of purely monumental work, we find the same capacity abundantly exemplified in the chaste specimens of polished marble, Aberdeen granite, freestone, and other specimens of memorial sculpture, all of which are possessed of an appropriateness of design and a beauty of outline and finish which we have never seen excelled. An additional display of highly wrought busts, figures, entablatures, etc., may be viewed in Mr. Wilson's admirably appointed show-rooms, where he maintains also an extensive and carefully selected stock of carved and polished marble mantels, and the like. In this portion of the premises, too, are the offices. The works, which immediately adjoin the show-rooms, comprise an excellent range of workshops capitally adapted to the purposes in hand, and finding employment for several experienced workmen, under the personal supervision of Mr. Wilson, who, needless to say, devotes direct attention to all work of importance. Some very noteworthy productions have been turned out from this establishment for ecclesiastical decorations, a notable instance being the beautiful Caen stone altar with carved figures, at present in the Berwick Roman Catholic Chapel. Many beautiful examples of

MONUMENTAL WORKS, BRIDGE END.

Mr. Wilson's work are also to be met with in all the cemeteries throughout the district, including a very fine monument erected to the memory of the late Mr. Thomas Allan, J.P., who, prior to his decease, was a member of the firm, who took it over in 1883. Its general progress has been of the most gratifying character.

## Mr. James Campbell, The Black Swan Hotel, Tweed Street.

The resources of an important centre like Berwick-on-Tweed could scarcely be considered complete unless they included a comfortable and thoroughly well managed hotel. Such an establishment is distinctly forthcoming in the shape of the reputable hostelry conducted by Mr. James Campbell, and widely known as the "Black Swan." The house in question was established so far back as 1770, passing into the present hands about twelve years ago. In 1894, the premises were entirely rebuilt at considerable cost, and as they stand to-day they undoubtedly constitute one of the most commodious and admirably appointed hotels in the north. The site, too, is an exceptionally central one, being immediately opposite Berwick Railway Station, and consequently within easy distance of the principal attractions of the locality; whilst the interior accommodation, comprising spacious coffee and commercial-rooms, stock-rooms, private sitting-rooms, a suitable bath-room, lavatory, range of bed-rooms, and bar with cosy smoke-room in the rear, commanding a fine view of the Tweed, has been fitted and furnished on the most up-to-date lines throughout. Excellent stabling is available at the rear, so that market day visitors, and parties driving into the town, will find their requirements equally well catered for. We need scarcely say that the entire arrangements are of a decidedly first class character. A liberal *cuisine* is maintained, the wines, beers, spirits, cigars, etc., are of the best possible quality, and the service, tariff and general *menage*, can scarcely fail to give

# 1994

## A & J ROBERTSON (GRANITE) LIMITED

### 1894 onwards

| | |
|---|---|
| 1897 | John Wilson - stone carver, monumental mason, marble and stone masons, Tweedside stone and marble works. |
| 1914 | John Wilson and Son - monumental masons, Bridge End, Tweedmouth. |
| 1938 | John Wilson and Son - monumental masons, Bridge End. |
| 1943 | Business purchased by George Sutherland and Son, Sculptors of Galashiels but still traded under name John Wilson and Son. |
| 1986 | A & J Robertson (Granite) Limited - monumental masons. |

In 1943 George Sutherland and Son, Sculptors purchased John Wilson's monumental masonry business in Tweedmouth. The business was to be run by John Sutherland, a younger son of the owner, David Sutherland, but tragically he was killed in the Second World War. A manager then ran the business on the firm's behalf until July 1986 when Sutherlands sold it to A & J Robertson (Granite) Limited.

A & J Robertson is a large company with branches in Edinburgh, Ayr and Aberdeen as well as Tweedmouth. One person is employed at Tweedmouth full time whilst letter cutters and teams for erecting headstones are brought in from other locations as required. The company make memorial vases and gravestones.

### Goods Sold

Memorial Headstone : £200 to £3000
Memorial Vase: £52 upwards

### Opening Hours

Monday - Friday : 9.30 am to 12.30 pm;
1.30 pm to 4.30 pm

## CASTLEGATE CARPETS

### 1894 Onwards

| | |
|---|---|
| 1897 | James Campbell - Black Swan |
| 1902 | Harris Baker - Black Swan Hotel |
| 1905 | John George Heavisides - Railway Inn |
| 1925 | William Thompson - motor car dealer and repairer, Station Garage |
| 1934 | William Thompson and Sons - Station Garage |
| 1969 | J. Todrick - garage and filling station |
| 1973 | Station garage - Alfred Flannigan |
| 1980 | Cash Carry Carpets - Alfred Flannigan |

# 1994

## CASTLEGATE CARPETS

Mr Flannigan, the present owner of the premises, originally operated a garage from here but in 1980 he changed his business to selling carpets. Two people work part time in the shop which sells a wide range of carpets.

**Opening Hours**
Monday - Saturday: 9.00 am to 6.00 pm

**Goods Sold**
Carpets: £1.99 per square yard upwards

## BRIDGE STREET CAR PARK

### 1894 onwards

| | |
|---|---|
| 1897 | John Robert Brough - wholesale and retail wine, spirit and bottled beer merchant and aerated water manufacturer. |
| 1902 | Ralph Bradford - wine and spirit merchant |
| 1906 | Old Hen and Chickens Inn has changed name to "Ye Old Bridge Tavern - Licensee : Ellias Hartley Haworth |
| 1910 | Licensee : Robert Sterling |
| 1959 | Licensee : Jean Sterling |
| 1963 | Premises demolished for construction of car park |

the utmost satisfaction to travellers of all sorts and conditions. Mr. James Campbell, the proprietor, has long been highly popular, both amongst his patrons and in local circles. He is a prominent member of the Berwick Town Council, and owing to the fact of his being the youngest representative hitherto returned to that body, is sometimes facetiously dubbed "The Baby Councillor." He has also identified himself with the Berwick Lodge of Royal Arch Free Masons, and acts as Trustee of the Old Society of Ancient Shepherds, besides taking an active interest in the Berwick Mechanics' Institute, and Cricket and Rowing Clubs.

THE BLACK SWAN HOTEL.

### Mr. John R. Brough,
### Wine and Spirit Merchant, Manufacturer of Aerated Waters, &c., Bridge Street.

No person is better known in connection with the wine and spirit trade in Berwick-on-Tweed than Mr. John R. Brough, who has built up an extensive and influential connection in this department, reaching to all parts of the border counties. Mr. Brough, who had had previous experience in the trade, came to Berwick in 1868, and joined the staff of the Border Brewery Company. He first started as a traveller for this well known concern, but his conspicuous business abilities speedily brought him promotion, and he was appointed manager of the brewery, a post that he held for eleven years. Ten years ago he determined to start upon his own account, and purchased the property which he now occupies, including the old "Hen and Chickens," a noted tavern, and one of the first to bear a name which has since been extensively used by other licensed houses. The premises, which are situated in Bridge Street, cover a considerable area of ground, running a long distance to the rear. They comprise bottling stores, commodious cellars, and a large mineral water factory. They are admirably organised and

THE OLD "HEN AND CHICKENS," BRIDGE STREET.

YARD AND MINERAL WATER FACTORY.

arranged throughout, the latest and most approved labour-saving appliances being in use in the bottling stores. Mr. Brough is agent for Worthington's pale ales, and also deals with the products of all the leading breweries, supplying them in bottle, cask, or barrel. He has also a splendid stock of spirits, from the most famous distilleries, all in a thoroughly matured condition. He imports his wines direct from the leading continental shippers, and holds many bins of the most renowned vintages; in addition, he is sole agent in Berwick for Max Greger's (Ltd.) celebrated Hungarian wines, as supplied to Her Majesty the Queen. Connoisseurs would do well to study his lists, since they contain particulars of many rare old wines, which are offered at exceptionally moderate prices. He has also extensive bonded stores for both wines and spirits. The mineral water factory is quite a model of what such an establishment should be. It is filled with a new plant of the most modern type, and is maintained in a state of scrupulous cleanliness. Only the purest ingredients are used in the process of manufacture, and the products of the factory are very highly esteemed, alike for their wholesome and palatable qualities. In the wholesale department Mr. Brough's intimate knowledge of the trade has enabled him to build up a most valuable connection, extending among the largest dealers in all the border districts. This department of the business is still rapidly increasing under Mr. Brough's able and enterprising management. For some four years after Mr. Brough came into possession of the property, the "Hen and Chickens" was in the hands of a lessee, and he occupied as his wine office a shop previously in the possession of a butcher. Now, however, he manages himself the retail as well as the wholesale department, and the "Hen and Chickens" has become one of the most popular and best conducted licensed houses in Berwick. Mr. Brough is assisted in the business by his son, Mr. J. I. Brough, who travels over the whole district, and under whose particular charge the aërated water manufactory is. Coming from the business to the social aspect of our subject, which, of course, forms a part of our programme in a review of this description, we may mention that Mr. Brough was elected a member of the Town Council for the South Ward some four years back. He now represents the Tweedmouth division on the Council. In these public offices he has displayed a most lively solicitude for the public welfare, and his eminent business abilities have been found of the highest services alike by his colleagues on the Council and by his fellow townsmen.

## Mr. W. A. Logan, Wine Merchant, Hide Hill.

In Berwick-upon-Tweed there are several wine merchants on whose selection implicit reliance may be placed, and among them Mr. W. A. Logan. His business is the oldest in its special line in the ancient border town, its foundation dating back to 1816, when it was established by a Mr. Henry Johnson, by whom it was carried on for many years. Subsequently it was acquired by Mr. David Logan, during whose administration its sphere of operation was considerably widened. Mr. David Logan eventually retired in favour of his son, the present sole proprietor, and is now busily occupied in his public life, being a Justice of the Peace and a Commissioner of Income Tax. Mr. W. A. Logan has had a long acquaintance with the special class of trade with which this business has been associated, and well upholds the strong position taken up by his predecessors. The office and order department, cellars and bottling department, are in Hide Hill. The premises present a good double frontage opposite Woods and Co.'s Bank. They extend to a considerable depth at the rear, and have admirable cellarage accommodation in the basement. In Silver Street Mr. Logan has Duty Free Stores, where large stocks of wines and spirits are kept, and where his blending operations are carried on; while in Pakes's Lane are the Beer and Stout Bottling Stores. The stock of wines and spirits is very extensive, and, amongst others, there are the most popular vintages of port and sherry wines. Champagnes by Giesler, Moët and Chandon, Ayala and Bernard are always kept on hand, and Mr. Logan's connection with other shippers enables him to promptly procure any special brand that may be desired. The various hocks and clarets make a very valuable and representative stock, while in whisky, rum, brandy, and gin the house is second to none in the county.

HIDE HILL.

# 1994

## BRIDGE STREET CAR PARK

In June 1963, Ye Olde Bridge Tavern, owned by Berwick Breweries Limited was demolished to make way for the present Bridge Street Car Park. Whilst demolition work was in progress, a Tudor Wall painting was discovered behind an old fireplace in one of the back rooms. Work was stopped and the wall painting, one of the few surviving examples in the country, was rescued and restored. The painting is now on display in the Borough Museum and Art Gallery in the Barracks.

Ye Old Bridge Tavern was commonly known by locals as "Smokey Joes" and was run by the same family for over 50 years. When Robert Stirling died, the licence was taken over by his daughter, Jean, who was there until the pub closed in 1963.

## CAFE PIZZAZ

### 1894 onwards

1897    William Archbold Logan - wholesale wine, spirit and bottled beer merchant

1914    William D. McColgan - hairdresser (35 Hide Hill)

1934    William D. McColgan - hairdresser

1939    William D. McColgan - barber

On the closure of William McColgan's business, the building became part of the Kings Arms Hotel. Today it is known as Cafe Pizzaz, serving Italian food, but in the past it has been the Georgian Inn (1978), Brambles Bistro (1980) and the Hideaway Restaurant (1990).

### Prices
Garlic Bread:                £1.45
Spaghetti alla Napolitana:   £3.95
Lasagne al Forno :           £4.95
Pizza Quatro Stagioni:       £5.30

### Opening Hours
Monday - Sunday:    11.00 am to 11.00 pm

# 1994

## POPINJAYS

### 1894 onwards

1897     John Elliott - agricultural chemist, aerated water and sheep dip manufacturer, oil and provision merchant, dry salter and tallow chandler.

1902     Executors of John Elliott

1914     Thomas Elliott - chemist

1936     Thomas Elliott - chemist and optician

1960     J.Booth - grocer

1973     J.Booth closed business

1974     Captain Philips' Corner Coffee Shop - Proprietors : Michael and Julie Esther

1977     Popinjays - Proprietor : Georgina Home Robertson

The building was constructed in 1718/19 by Captain Thomas Philips, the engineer appointed to oversee the construction of the Barracks. The remains of the original stables can still be seen in the courtyard at the back of the premises where furnishing fabric is sold. Today the premises is a busy and popular cafe offering customers anything from a cup of coffee to a cooked meal. Five people are employed in the cafe full time as well as three part time and eight weekend staff. The cafe's name "Popinjays" is derived from an old word for "parrot" which forms part of the Home of Wedderburn crest.

### Opening Hours

Monday - Saturday :     9.30 am to 5.00 pm
Sunday :     11.00 am to 5.00 pm

### Goods Sold

Cooked Meal :     £3.75
Sandwich :     £1.20
Scone:     £0.60

Foreign liqueurs of every kind are on hand, and the assortment of aerated waters, Australian wines, and British cordials, etc., is of a high degree of excellence. A speciality is made of Raggett's Golden Hop Pale Ale and Nourishing Stout, for which Mr. Logan is the sole agent in Berwick. Referring to these, Dr. Hassell, M.D., says, "I find them to be as fine in quality as any beers that have of late years come under my notice, combining the flavour and fragrance of the best malt and hops. This uniform standard of excellence which I have observed for more than a quarter of a century enables me to report most highly as to their dietetic value." This opinion by the analyst of the *Lancet* Sanitary Commission cannot fail to ensure a continuance of the high favour in which these goods have always been held. Bass and Co.'s well known productions are also on hand, and in the same connection it may be mentioned that Mr. Logan is the local agent for Newsome Baxter's Northallerton Ales.

## Mr. John Elliot,
### Wholesale, Retail Manufacturing and Agricultural Chemist, Manufacturer of Sheep and Lamb Dipping Composition, Tallow Chandler, Oil and Colourman, and Aerated Water Manufacturer, Hide Hill.

The above comprehensive business, which was established by the present proprietor in 1844, and will attain its jubilee in August of the present year, occupies a position of distinct importance in the Border capital, both as a family pharmacy and in connection with the manufacture and supply of veterinary medicaments, sheep dips, and specialities for cage birds, etc., which have for years past been in high repute throughout the district. The principal items put forward under the head referred to include the sheep rearing interest over forty years and is exclusively used by the most eminent flockmasters in the border counties; and Elliot's Special Bird Foods and Medicines, comprising Egg Bread, Inga Seed, Canarydine Bread, Bird Seed and Fruit Mixture, Bird Tonic, Vitalized Oil, Lark Mixture, Blackbird and Thrush Food, Bird Gravel, Liquid Insect Destroyer, and Avepers for colouring canaries a rich deep orange whilst moulting. In addition to the foregoing, Mr. Elliot keeps on hand the whole round of reliable proprietary medicines for horses, cattle, sheep and dogs as prepared by the principal manufacturing houses identified with the trade, and conducts also the local agencies for Spratt's Patent Dog Biscuits and Simpson's Cattle Spice. He further devotes careful attention to the supply of complete veterinary medicine chests for farm, stud, and professional use; the preparation

HIDE HILL.

Elliot's Condition Powder for Horses, an alterative and tonic medicine of especial value in cases of grease, swelled legs, and all affections of the skin; Elliot's Cleansing Drink, invariably found most efficacious for removing the "cleansing" and restoring the condition of cows after calving; Elliot's Black Vulnerary Oil, for allaying swellings, inflammation, sprains, bruises, relaxed sinews, warbles, galled back, sore throats, and wounds of every description; Elliot's Driffield Oil, recommended for sheep after difficult lambing; Elliot's Red Mixture, for feverish and inflammatory affections after lambing; Elliot's Spasmodic Tincture, unrivalled in cases of batts or gripes in the horse; Elliot's Golden Ointment, specially adapted to the treatment of bony enlargements in horses; Elliot's Tonic Restorative Balls, for horses and neat cattle; Elliot's Astringent Powders for calves, a never-failing remedy for violent purging; Elliot's Sheep and Lamb Dipping Composition, which has been before of medicines in accordance with veterinary prescriptions, and the manufacture of special dips, baths, etc., to suit individual requirements. The premises in which the business is carried on are centrally situated at Hide Hill, immediately opposite the King's Arms Hotel, and within easy distance of the Cattle Market and the railway station. They consist of a spacious double fronted warehouse, well furnished and appointed throughout with every requisite for the work of the sale and dispensing departments. In the rear also are commodious stores for reserve stocks, together with ample convenience for conducting the manufacturing operations under the best possible auspices. The assortments of goods embrace the most reliable qualities of drugs and chemicals, medical and surgical appliances, toilet requisites, hygienic and therapeutic agents and vehicles, patent medicines and proprietary articles of all kinds, perfumery, mineral waters, tallow and wax candles, oils, colours and varnishes, and druggists' sundries of every description. The dispensing department is carefully and skilfully conducted under the immediate supervision of the proprietor. Special attention is given to the execution of country orders, which, owing to the facilities afforded by the Parcel Post, can be made up and despatched the same day as received, and any article not in stock is promptly obtained when required. As one of the oldest practitioners on the Tweed side, Mr. Elliot deservedly enjoys the confidence and support of a wide circle of professional and private clients.

## Messrs. W. and J. Hogarth, Butchers, 85, High Street.

It is no exaggeration to say that the general gustatory and elementary requirements of Berwick are catered for with more than ordinary adequacy, and as regards the matter of fresh meat, residents may reasonably congratulate themselves on the fact that they have amongst them several firms of butchers who can be invariably relied upon to supply a really first class article on thoroughly satisfactory terms. One of the leading houses associated with the interest referred to is undoubtedly that of Messrs. W. and J. Hogarth, who, after acquiring considerable experience as family butchers in their late establishment at Bridge Street, some eight years ago

85, HIGH STREET.

purchased the old established business formerly carried on by Mr. Robert Wood. The enterprise in question dates from the year 1810, and may consequently claim to be the oldest butchery business in the town. Messrs. Hogarth have spared neither energy nor resource in bringing it up to its present condition of efficiency—a circumstance which, to say the least of it, fully entitles them to the augmented share of influential patronage they at present enjoy. The premises, situated in Berwick's main thoroughfare, viz:— High Street, are exceedingly commodious and exceptionally well ventilated, and as nothing but prime ox beef, good Wether mutton, and the best of pork, veal, and lamb in season are put forward, it is no wonder that the concern is largely patronised by the better class of consumers. Both principals are expert judges of live meat, and invariably make judicious selections, as is proved by the unvarying quality, not to say superiority, of the supplies they place on sale. The establishment is further noted as a centre from which fresh mince and sausages may be obtained daily, the latter delicacies being expressly made on the premises from the most wholesome meat, cut up by an improved "Williams" mincing machine, driven by gas power. Corned beef, pickled tongues, rounds, etc. are also supplied, together with home cured hams and bacon, for all of which the firm sustain a high reputation. Town and country orders are delivered with the utmost promptitude, a large trade being done both amongst private families and the local hotels and institutions. Messrs. Hogarth devote great care and attention to their business, and take the utmost pains to give every purchaser the full benefit of the resources at command. As throwing additional light on the secret of their indubitable success, we may mention in conclusion that in connection with the High Street establishment, they farm upwards of 200 acres of land at Edrington Castle, which land is exclusively set apart for grazing and fattening cattle and sheep, prior to their being killed for sale.

## Mr. J. J. Simmen, French and English Cook, Confectioner, & Pastry Baker, 31, Bridge Street.

Mr. J. J. Simmen's establishment in Bridge Street is a decided acquisition to Berwick-on-Tweed. It consists of a well fitted double fronted shop, with private refreshment

31, BRIDGE STREET.

room and confectionery making premises at the rear. Mr. Simmen, formerly of Hawick, was erstwhile head confectioner with the Queen's Restaurant Purveying Co., Buchanan Street, Glasgow, and is a perfect artist at his craft. Besides being a French and English cook, pastry baker, and confectioner, he is a purveyor of wedding breakfasts, dinners, ball suppers, soirées, &c., and also is a noted maker of bride cakes. At the restaurant in Bridge Street hot dinners are provided on Saturdays; and during the summer season, for the convenience of Spittal visitors, Mr. Simmen conducts a well appointed refreshment-room in Main Street, at the first entrance to the promenade. Estimates are given for catering for pic-nics, school trips, and the like, visiting Berwick-on-Tweed or Spittal. Mr. Simmen's experience at home and abroad has been varied and extensive, and his taste is cosmopolitan and delicate. He is the original maker of the famed almond cuts in the border burghs. The business has been established 10 years. *Man spricht Deutch. On parle Française.*

# 1994

## GREENWOODS

### 1894 onwards

| | |
|---|---|
| 1897 | Walter and John Hogarth - butchers |
| 1914 | Walter and John Hogarth - butchers |
| 1925 | Robert George White - butchers |
| 1955 | Robert George White - butchers (Proprietor : Mrs M.Rutherford ) |
| 1962 | Rocket Men's Shop - menswear |
| 1972 | Anthony Donald Ltd. - menswear |
| 1979 | Greenwoods - menswear |

Butchers operated from these premises for almost 150 years before the building was taken over by the Rocket Shop in the early 1960s. Today the shop is occupied by Greenwoods, a national chain of menswear shops. It employs one full time and one part time member of staff.

### Opening Hours
Monday - Saturday:    9.30 am - 5.30 pm

### Goods Sold
| | |
|---|---|
| Trousers: | £21.99 |
| Sweaters: | £24.99 |
| Suits: | £125.00 |

## OLD BRIDGE CRAFTS

### 1894 onwards

| | |
|---|---|
| 1897 | John Jacob Simmen - confectioner |
| 1906 | George Todd - musical instrument dealer |
| 1914 | Board of Trade Labour Exchange |
| 1929 | Ministry of Labour Employment Exchange (manager - Robert Topping ) |
| 1934 | Robert Henry Dawson Knox - antique dealer |
| 1975 | John Roberts - antique shop |
| 1978 | Wojtek and Irena - ladies' and gents' Hair Saloon |
| 1990 | Antique shop |

Mr Marshall opened his shop, Old Bridge Crafts, in 1992. He works there himself restoring and hand painting old furniture and has a part time assistant to help him. In the shop he sells various crafts including dried flower arrangements, wrought iron work, wooden shelves and hand painted kitchen artefacts.

### Opening Hours
Monday - Saturday :   9.30 am to 4.00 pm (Winter)
                      9.30 am to 5.30 pm (Summer)
                      On Thursdays closes at 1 pm

### Goods Sold
| | |
|---|---|
| Hand painted wooden chairs : | £20.00 to £30.00 |
| Hand painted pots : | £1.49 to £8.99 |

# 1994

## KING JAMES' COURT

### 1894 onwards

1897    Alexander Henderson - bookseller, stationer and stamp distributor

1906    Alexander Henderson and Son - bookseller and stationer

1929    A.Henderson and Son - stationers

1934    Jack's Furniture Stores - furniture dealers (Proprietor : Jack Levinson )

1953    The Modern Cafe - lunches, teas and suppers (Proprietors : R & A Palmer and Son )

1962    Irvine Electrical Service Limited

In the late 1970s the shop, along with other premises in West Street, was demolished to make way for a sheltered housing complex for elderly people. This complex, known as King James' Court was built for Anchor Housing Association by Stanley Miller. It cost £350,000 and was opened in April 1979. Within the building there are 22 single and 7 double flats as well as various communal areas. A warden lives on the premises to ensure the welfare of the tenants.

**Rent Charge**
Single :   £231.02 per calendar month
Double : £252.39 per calendar month

## Messrs. A. Henderson and Son,
### Booksellers, Stationers, Bookbinders, and Printers, 42, West Street.

MR. A. HENDERSON.

As the bookshops of a town are unquestionably the truest index to the general character and tastes of its inhabitants, it is only appropriate that they should be well represented in the best parts of Berwick, and the handsome shop of Mr. A. Henderson, trading as "A. Henderson and Son," is well deserving of the prominent position which has been allotted to it. The premises, with their extensive frontage and well dressed windows, form a conspicuous ornament to West Street, between High Street and Bridge Street, and occupy one of the best positions in the town. The business was established by Mr. A. Henderson, senr., as far back as 1848, his son—also Mr.

that the printing executed by Messrs. Henderson is artistic, and bears evidence of their having at command the most perfect modern type and machinery; the bookbinding is also executed in the highest style of the art. A very large and comprehensive selection of works of history, travel, fiction, poetry, science, etc., by standard authors, and school books is kept in stock; of Bibles, Prayer Books, Hymn Books, and devotional works there is also a very superior collection in various styles of binding. This is the local depot of the Society for Promoting Christian Knowledge, and any of the numerous publications of this Society can be obtained on short notice. The assortment of commercial, scholastic, and plain and fancy stationery is an eminently good one, including all the favourite makes of paper and envelopes; while in English and foreign fancy goods the stock is very large, and comprises bags, purses, jewel boxes, handkerchief and glove boxes, inkstands, date racks, candlesticks, writing desks, leather writing cases, ladies' companions, lined work baskets, photo frames, albums, gongs; and there is also here a fine selection of photographic views of local and other scenery by Valentine and other well known artists. A

42, WEST STREET.

A. Henderson—succeeding to it about ten years ago, after having been for some considerable time the junior partner in the concern. The mechanical departments include lithography, engraving, letterpress and commercial printing, bookbinding, and the manufacture of ledgers and every description of account books to order, and it is not too much to say that the wide range that the operations of the house cover, and the comprehensive nature of the work that the firm are always prepared to undertake, render the commercial portion of Berwick entirely self-dependent in these respects. In fact, there is not the slightest necessity for customers to look to Newcastle, Edinburgh, or any other place for their supplies as long as they come within the limits of Messrs. A. Henderson and Son's trade, as the firm are prepared to fulfil orders equal in quality and price to any of their competitors, and obviously with less delay than generally arises from having work done at a distance. We may mention in particular

particularly interesting souvenir of the town in the shape of an album containing twenty-four views of local scenery is published here. The peculiar richness of the neighbourhood in points of interest renders the task of selecting any special twenty-four a rather difficult one, but the album referred to meets the difficulty well, and being nicely bound in cloth and sold at the moderate price of 1s., tourists have at their hand one of the most interesting reminders of a pleasant trip that they could desire. In addition to the departments mentioned, Mr. Henderson has a large general trade, and supplies newspapers, books, magazines and periodicals to several public institutions in the town and neighbourhood, and he also conducts a general advertising business in connection with the local, London, and provincial papers. Mr. Henderson, who is moderate in his charges throughout, conducts his business with much energy and success, and he well deserves the large amount of patronage with which he is favoured.

## Mr. William Green, Photographer, 9, Castlegate.

The views of Berwick, which we have produced, and most of the portraits in these columns, are from photographs by Mr. William Green. This gentleman has brought the permanent carbon or autotype process to a very high state of perfection, and he employs it in every phase of photography with marked success. Some very beautiful examples of his out-door work are shown in a set of beautiful cloud negatives, designed to fill in the skyground of views—very simple instructions for using these being supplied in several languages for the convenience of foreign artists. Another notable speciality is a series of photos of birds, their nests and breeding places, taken from life, and most valuable from a natural history point of view. Of the same character is a series of Chillingham wild cattle, and a set of six fine etchings in sepia of Norham, Twizel, Berwick, Holy Island and Bamboro'.

## Mr. George Smith, Cycle Agent, Plumber, Hardware Merchant, and Sanitary Engineer, 74, Main Street, Tweedmouth.

At the near approach of another season, when once more the fraternity of wheelmen will be flying over the highways of the country, it may be well to remind this numerous section of the public that ample provision is made for their requirements at the popular establishment of Mr. George Smith, cycle agent and hardware merchant, who has with his usual enterprise laid in a large stock of machines by all the leading makers for the benefit of his wide circle of clients. This gentleman has now been engaged in this business for some nine years past, and having the fullest experience of the trade, has built up a very substantial business in this line in each department indicated at the head of this notice. The establishment, centrally situated at 74, Main Street (opposite the Dock, and near Old Berwick Bridge) consists of a spacious and

TWEEDSIDE CYCLE DEPOT.

well appointed shop and warehouse, affording every convenience for the storage and display of goods incidental to the business. First in importance must be noted the admirable show of cycles. Mr. Smith is the local agent for such celebrated makes as Raleigh, Whitworth, Elswick, Raglan, Excelsior, Zenith and other machines. Mr. Smith's own special make, of which a new pattern just introduced will be one of the novelties of the season, is styled the "Borderer," an improved safety, fitted with dust proof bearings, balled in every part, and contains in the details of its construction new features intended to effect accelerated pace while adding to comfort in riding, for either road or racing purposes. This machine is supplied at a very moderate price on either the cash or hire system, and may be commended to intending purchasers as well worthy of their attention when selecting for the coming season. Cycles fitted with cushion or pneumatic tyres can be had at moderate charges by the hour, day, or week.

INTERIOR TWEEDSIDE CYCLE DEPOT.

Mr. Smith also holds large stocks of cycle accessories and fittings, and has every facility for the execution of repairs, which are carried out on the premises by experienced hands on the shortest notice at reasonable charges. Other items of the stock include every description of Birmingham and Sheffield goods and general hardware. In addition to the branches already enumerated, Mr. Smith undertakes general plumbing, electric bell fitting, and sanitary engineering, hot and cold water fitting, etc., employing competent and trustworthy men for each class of work. Executed under the personal supervision of the proprietor, the utmost dependence can be placed in the efficiency and thoroughly practical workmanship of all orders entrusted to him.

## Berwick Oil Mills.

The Berwick Oil Mills fulfil a distinctly important function in relation to the industrial economy of the district. Established so far back as the year 1860, they have represented the oil-cake interest in the north, ever since the time when farmers first commenced to recognise the value of cake as feeding stuff. The founder of the business was the late Mr. Matthew Young, a gentleman who, possessing considerably more than average business capabilities, has left behind a name and a reputation which are long likely to survive. A town councillor of fifteen years' standing, and an elder and trustee of Wallace Green Church, few men were more prominently identified with the public and religious affairs of the municipality, whilst his ability and *penchant* for enterprise undoubtedly helped him to build up one of the most valuable businesses associated with the locality. Since 1888 the Berwick Oil Mills have been successfully worked by Mr. Young's executors—the general management being in the hands of Mr. James T. Scott, whose intimate acquaintance with the details of the manufacture, have proved of material advantage to the proprietors. As at

# 1 9 9 4

## SPAR

### 1894 onwards

| | |
|---|---|
| 1897 | George Smith - plumber and cycle agent |
| 1906 | Mary and Isabella Logan - greengrocers |
| 1938 | Misses Mary and Isabella Logan - fruiterers |
| 1955 | T.W.Rea - grocer |
| 1963 | Vivo Self Service (T.W.Rea ) - licensed grocer |
| 1985 | Spar ( T.W.Rea ) - licensed grocer |

T.W.Rea has run his business from these premises since 1955. The shop, run as Spar, a national chain of small shops, is open from early morning to late at night. It sells various groceries, fruit and vegetables and also operates as an off licence. Two people are employed there full time as well 13 people on a part time basis.

### Opening Hours

Monday - Saturday : 8.00am to 10.00 pm
Sunday : 8.30am to 10.00 pm

### Goods Sold

| | |
|---|---|
| Heinz Baked Beans : | 29 pence |
| Mars Bar: | 26 pence |
| Kelloggs Cornflakes (500 g ) : | £1.15 |
| Butter (250g ): | 71 pence |
| 20 Regal Kingsize cigarettes : | £2 .67 |

# 1994

## CLOTHESLINE CLASSIC

### 1894 onwards

1897   Francis Mason - baker and confectioner

1914   Peter Mason - baker and confectioner

1934   James Ironside - florist, seedsman and fruiterer

1969   Ironsides - florists

1975   The Flower Shop - florist

1993   Clothesline Classic - women's clothes shop

After operating as a flower shop for over 50 years, these premises had a change of use in 1993 when Clothesline Classic opened. The business is owned by Meg Dudgeon and sells ladieswear - skirts, dresses, suits, blouses. Three women work in the shop on a part time basis. Clothesline also has another shop in Hide Hill which sells casual clothes for women and children.

### Opening Hours
Monday - Saturday :   9.30 am to 5.00 pm

### Goods Sold
Skirts :            £21.00 upwards
Blouses :           £21.00 upwards
Jacket :            £44.00 upwards

present organised, the mills are contained in a substantial building some 300ft. by 100ft., giving ample storage accommodation for cake seed and oil, and facilities for producing about twelve tons of cake per day, with oil in proportion. The works are fitted with hydraulic presses by Rose, Downes and Thompson, of Hull; the plant includes nine capacious tanks, in which upwards of 104 tons of oil can be stored at one time. The entire manufacture is conducted under auspices which are calculated to secure uniformity and unfluctuating excellence of output. The goods are made from the finest pure linseed, and are noted for quality on all the northern markets. The linseed-cake is attested as high class by the leading chemists, and commands a high price. Their feeding compound cake is useful for all kinds of stock, and a cotton-cake is made from the finest Egyptian seed. The other products are bruised linseed for calf-rearing, linseed oil for horses, and for the general market. The feeding stuffs are mostly sold in the Border counties, where they are in general demand. The linseed oil finds a market in London, Glasgow, Newcastle-on-Tyne, &c., where it commands exceptional prices on account of its purity and fine quality. On the whole the Berwick Oil Mills may be described as one of the essentially useful and prosperous undertakings of the Border counties.

## Mr. Francis Mason,
### Bread, Biscuit and Pastry Baker and Confectioner, 2, Church Street.

The baker is in the enviable position of being an absolutely essential tradesman to any community, and though the trade has, like others, its special difficulties to encounter, a man who supplies the public with pure and wholesome bread, is pretty certain of a fair measure of support. Some, of course, attain more than this, and the proprietor of the business of which we are now writing is an example of this. It was established many years back by Mr. Thomas Houliston, who retired in 1848, and now occupied by Mr. Francis Mason. Though, by long experience, well versed in all branches of the baking and confectionery trade, and competent in the production of the various articles connected therewith, it has been the aim of Mr Mason to continue the study and improve the art of bread-making. In this way, besides making a very superior kind of plain household bread, he produces all kinds of fancy bread of a light delicate and nutritious flavour. He is also known as a manufacturer of Oliver's Patent Wholemeal Brown Bread, which was used in the Dairy Department of the Health Exhibition, and which is so strongly recommended by the faculty.

These goods are delivered daily to all parts of Berwick and district, many of the best classes of residents being among the permanent and regular patrons of the house. Mr. Mason's reputation is, however, by no means confined to the limits of the old Border town. He sends real Scotch oat cakes and Scotch shortbread to all parts of the world. Specialities of the business are Ginger-bread and Madeira, Seed, Plum, Pound, Cherry, and other cakes, toothsome confections, which must be tried to be appreciated. Wedding, christening, birthday, Christmas and New Year cakes are made, and in this connection a wide reputation has been gained. Many varieties of wine and luncheon biscuits are made, and all kinds of plain and fruit cakes. In the lighter forms of confectionery Mr. Mason has achieved a marked success with his jellies, ices and creams, and these goods are largely supplied to wedding, birthday, and other festivities, catering for which is an important branch of the business. The premises are extensive, and are situated at the rear of the Town Hall, and comprise a well appointed double fronted shop, bakehouse and stores. Throughout the entire place the perfection of cleanliness and good order is maintained. The ingredients used in the course of manufacture are fresh and pure, and the house has a reputation for the high standard of excellence attained in every article emanating from it.

2, CHURCH STREET.

## Messrs. Thompson Brothers,
### General & Furnishing Ironmongers, Iron, Metal, Oil & Paint Merchants, China, Glass & Earthenware Dealers, 41 & 43, High Street.

The extent and comprehensiveness of Messrs. Thompson Brothers render it a very important feature in the resources of modern Berwick. Both partners are practical men, with a long experience in the trade, and the relations the firm have formed with some of the leading producers enable them to lay in stock on very favourable terms, and to supply high class reliable goods at moderate prices. The improvements constantly taking place in lamps, stoves, and similar goods, are always represented in the stock of the firm, and novelties are being introduced every day. The business was established in 1875, by Mr. Thomas Thompson, the present senior partner, who was subsequently joined in partnership by his brother, Mr. Burnett Greive Thompson, these two now forming the firm. close by are spacious stores for heavy iron in bar and sheet, of which large supplies are held. Messrs. Thompson do a good trade in sporting guns, of which they hold a very fine selection, embracing all the most recent improvements as to lightness, security, rapid firing and accuracy, as well as handsome finish. In connection with this department they hold a large stock of high class ammunition and accessories. The next department calling for special mention is the splendid series of show-rooms devoted to glass, china and earthenware. These goods represent the best productions of the leading firms in the kingdom. There are handsome breakfast, tea and dinner services in many choice designs, lovely vases, toilet sets, &c., and for those who have articles to be matched these show-rooms afford rare facilities, wine glasses, sugar basins, butter coolers, vases, epergnes, and many other varieties of goods in plain, cut, flint and ornamental glass are also held in surprising variety. On the opposite side of High Street they have very extensive stores and a

41 AND 43, HIGH STREET.

The premises in High Street are very commodious. They consist of a large, handsome double fronted shop, in a good position, and with great internal accommodation. There are eight spacious show-rooms, well lighted, and handsomely fitted, and they are all fully stocked with goods. The arrangement throughout is convenient and businesslike, and a competent staff is engaged, so that orders are executed promptly. The stock includes household ironmongery of all kinds, fenders, fire-irons, and brasses, tin, brass, and hollow-ware, toilet and japanned goods, &c., as well as cutlery, electro plate and silver goods, fancy brass ware, lamps for table, floor, and hall, and a very good line in ornamental mantel clocks. Builders' and general ironmongery are all well represented also in handsome chimney-pieces, overmantels, locks, tools, garden requisites, &c. In their oil and colour department the firm hold large stocks of the finest oils imported both for lighting, lubricating, painting and general purposes. All varieties of paints and varnishes for decorators, builders, and wood workers are kept, and handsome saloon, where ranges, open and close, fitted with all the latest improvements are on view. In this saloon are also shown laundry goods, dairy churns, lawn mowers, and an extensive collection of stoves with tiled panels, marble and enamelled mantel-pieces, and some very fine examples of hearth tiling. Underneath this saloon are the workshops and oil cellars of the firm, in the former of which a large staff of workmen are always fully employed making and repairing ironwork of every description, tin ware, &c., and generally executing everything in connection with the numerous branches of their trade. Special attention is given to the supplying and fitting up of bells, ranges, hot and cold water appliances, heating apparatuses for churches, public buildings, schools, green-houses, &c., Boyle's patent system of air pump ventilation, wire fencing, &c., estimates for which are given on application. The prices are unusually moderate, and the enterprise of the partners has met with a thorough public recognition in the substantial form of an extensive and increasing patronage.

# 1994

## GRANADA

### 1894 onwards

1897     Thompson Brothers - ironmongers

1914     Thompson Brothers - ironmongers
            Thomas Thompson - agent for Phoenix Assurance Co. Limited

1920     John Mosgrove - boot and shoemaker

1959     John Mosgrove - boot and shoemaker

1984     Tip Top Store Limited - drug store

1988     Clydesdale Retail Limited - electrical store

1994     Granada - change of name.

Granada, which took over from Clydesdale, opened in March 1994. It caters for the home entertainment market - renting and selling televisions, videos and satellite systems.

### Opening Hours
Monday - Saturday :     9.00 am to 5.00 pm.

### Goods Sold/ For Rent
21" Remote Control colour TV :    £9.99 rental per month
Video Recorder :                £9.99 rental per month
Ex Rental video recorder :        £99.99

# 1994

## AQUAMARINE JEWELLERS

Ralph Holmes and Sons operated their retail business from 34 - 36 Bridge Street until 1984 when the premises were taken over by Mr Aungier, jeweller. The shop, which employs three full time members of staff, sells and repairs all types of jewellery.

**Opening Hours**
Tuesday - Saturday : 9.30 am to 5.00 pm

## RALPH HOLMES AND SONS (FISH MERCHANTS) LIMITED

### 1894 onwards

| | |
|---|---|
| 1897 | Ralph Holmes and Sons - wholesale fish and game dealers |
| 1910 | Ralph Holmes and Sons - wholesale fish and game dealers, 32 - 36 Bridge Street |
| 1938 | Ralph Holmes and Sons - wholesale fishmongers, 32 - 36 Bridge Street |
| 1953 | Ralph Holmes and Sons - 32 Bridge Street |
| 1959 | Ralph Holmes and Sons - wholesale fishmongers, 34 + 36 Bridge Street |

This is the oldest surviving business in the town of Berwick and has been operating since 1780. It was started by Mr Ralph Smith, a wholesale and retail salmon, fish and game dealer and taken over by Ralph Holmes in November 1853. Since then the business has remained in the Holmes family, passing from father to son, to the present owner Ralph Holmes.

From these premises in Bridge Street, the business sells and dispatches all over the world salmon caught at its fisheries on the River Tweed. Depending on the season, up to 28 men are employed at the fisheries. As well as salmon, kippers are smoked and cured on the premises. In the 1980s, the shop moved from its 1894 premises (34 + 36), now Aquamarine Jewellers, to the present shop, No. 32. Bridge Street.

**Opening Hours**
Monday - Friday :   9.00 am to 1.00 pm;
                    2.00 pm to 5.00 pm
Saturday :          9.30 am to noon

**Goods Sold**
Smoked Salmon :     £8.50 per pound
Kippers :           £1.35 per pound

## Messrs. R. Holmes and Sons, Wholesale & Retail Salmon, Fish & Game Merchants, 34 and 36, Bridge Street.

The business at present controlled by Messrs. R. Holmes and Sons, is probably one of the oldest in Berwick, enterprise occupy a singularly advantageous site in Bridge Street, and consist of two spacious shops, the interiors of which have been thrown into one. The stock kept on hand necessarily varies in accordance with the season, but it is a well recognised fact that whatever is seasonable as regards either sea, fresh water or shell fish, game, wild fowl, etc.,

34 AND 36, BRIDGE STREET.

having been established in 1760. Its modern position is of the most influential character, for in addition to large dealings as retail fish and game merchants and purveyors to many of the leading families in the town and county, the firm maintain intimate relations with wholesale buyers, may always be obtained at Holmes's in the best condition, and on the most economical terms. The proprietors spare no endeavour to meet the convenience and behests of town and country customers alike in the most efficient and thoroughly enterprising manner, and to this end they have

INTERIOR, 34 AND 36, BRIDGE STREET.

WEIGHING AND CHECKING FISH.

being widely known on markets as lessees of an important salmon fishery. They contribute to the supply of Billingsgate, and are leaseholders of premises at Thurso, Wick, Skye, Dunbar, and St. Ives (Cornwall), so extensive are the ramifications of their trade. The head-quarters of the made special arrangements for dealing with orders received through the post or per wire, besides having organised a system of delivery whereby goods can be forwarded to any part of Berwick and its environs with the utmost promptitude. The firm make a speciality of boiling and parboiling salmon (the latter being recommended by the late D. F. R. Buckland), Tweedside fashion. We may mention that on the occasion of our visit some 70lbs. of salmon was being boiled for a local dinner. To the rear of the main premises Messrs. Holmes and Sons maintain extensive stores in connection with the wholesale department, and they have also commodious accommodation for fish curing, cleaning and general storage on the opposite side of Bridge Street. The principals take an active part in the management, personally supervising all details, and thereby retaining for the concern that reputation for efficiency and straightforward business methods which have hitherto stood it in such good stead.

Taken all round we know of no undertaking in Berwick more distinctly worthy of popular support; and it is, therefore, not surprising to find that in spite of its already substantial proportions the trade is still steadily on the increase.

## Mr. James Grey,
## Wine and Spirit Merchant, Hide Hill.

The business now carried on by Mr. James Grey, wine and spirit merchant, of Hide Hill, Berwick, was established about eighty-five years ago, and is consequently one of the oldest in the district. The original founder was the late Mr. Cockburn, whom the present proprietor succeeded in 1867. Of late years Mr. Grey has been ably assisted in the management by his two sons, Messrs. William and James Lilburn Grey—the latter gentleman devoting his main energies to the travelling—and under the co-direction a very extensive and important trade is conducted. The premises at Hide Hill exhibit exceptional suitability to the purposes in hand, occupying an advantageous site immediately opposite the Post Office and the Corn Exchange, and affording capital facilities for the maintenance of stock and the general transaction of business. They comprise well arranged order offices, with ample cellarage beneath, and bottling stores, etc., to the rear. The resources of the house further include commodious cellars and bottling accommodation in Old Brewery Lane—a thoroughfare abutting on Hide Hill—and also bonded warehouses in Silver Street. Views of the interior of the Hide Hill office and stores, and of one of the departments at Old Brewery Lane, accompany the present notice. In walking through the various cellars one is particularly struck by the magnitude and comprehensiveness of the selections

HIDE HILL.

of wines and spirits, liqueurs, etc., kept in stock, and taking into consideration the remarkable quality observable in every department, we cannot wonder that the concern is universally noted for the superiority of its goods. The more important lines on hand embrace numerous choice parcels of thoroughly matured vintage wines, shipped by the best firms associated with the interest, as well as one of the largest and most representative assortments of reliable whiskies and other spirits it has hitherto been our lot to come across. Mr. Grey makes a speciality

# 1994

## EDWIN THOMPSON AND COMPANY

### 1894 onwards

1897    James Grey - wine and spirit merchants

1902    James Grey and Sons - wine and spirit merchants

1938    James Grey and Sons - wine and spirit merchants

1952    Fisons Limited - fertiliser manufacturers

1959    H.G.McCreath and Co. Limited - seed merchants
        Royal Insurance Co. Limited.

1985    Edwin Thompson and Company - chartered surveyors; land and commercial agents

James Grey and Sons, the wine and spirit merchants, appear to have ceased trading just before the outbreak of the Second World War. After this the building was used by Fisons and then H.G.McCreath, before it was purchased by Edwin Thompson and Company in 1985. From these offices, the company operates as chartered surveyors, land and commercial agents throughout North Northumberland and the Borders. The services they offer include commercial and residential property valuation; property sales; building designs; supervision of Works as well as rural estate, farm, forestry and woodland management. The business is owned by five partners and there are also offices in Carlisle, Galashiels and Keswick. The Berwick office employs eight full time and one part time member of staff.

### Opening Hours

Monday - Friday :    9.00 am to 5.30 pm
Saturday :           9.00 am to 12.30 pm

# 1994

## EDWIN THOMPSON AND COMPANY

of a particularly fine old Scotch whiskey, which is blended on the premises, and could scarcely be surpassed in the matters of softness, flavour, and in fact the whole round of desirable qualities a thoroughly good whiskey should possess. Very excellent value is likewise put forward with respect to sherries, clarets, chateau wines, hocks, moselle, Madeira, etc., whilst as regards ports, it is not too much to say that for both *connoisseurs* and ordinary consumers unusually adequate provision is made. We need scarcely add that under the head of wines, liqueurs and spirits alike, Mr. Grey does a very substantial trade, the connection being largely amongst private families and

OFFICES.

BOTTLING CELLARS.

hotels, and extending to all the country round. Considerable bottling operations are carried on, and we may here note that in addition to procuring his supplies of ale, stout, etc., from the most important breweries in the kingdom, the proprietor exercises careful supervision over the work of bottling *per se*, so as to ensure the utmost efficiency, and the delivery of goods in the soundest and brightest condition. In view of the facts stated it is not surprising to find that the enterprise enjoys the confidence of an exceptionally influential circle of supporters, and that the

PACKING-ROOM.

business continues to show steady increases in volume from year to year. No endeavour is spared to keep well abreast of high class requirements, and to foster by every legitimate means that *prestige* which the concern has retained for so many years past, and we have consequently much pleasure in recommending the undertaking thus briefly reviewed, to the continued confidence of the local public. A large trade is done in the south of England. Agent: Mr. John Grey, Rozel, Lansdowne Road, South Woodford, Essex; and of Messrs. Mann, Crossman, and Paulin, Mile End Road, London.

## Boston Brothers, Fish Curers, Spittal.

The business conducted under the above style was originally founded about fifty years ago by the late Councillor Robert Boston, who carried it on with marked capacity and success down to the time of his death, three years ago. Since Mr. Boston's demise affairs have been directed by his three sons, Messrs. Robert, Peter P., and James Boston, whose experience of the trade goes without saying. The Berwick premises occupy an exceptionally advantageous site at Spittal, near the mouth of the river Tweed, and in convenient proximity to the railway station. They consist of extensive yards, with commodious curing, smoking, and kippering sheds, and a well equipped cooperage. During the season the firm frequently employ over a hundred hands, male and female, and some idea of the general magnitude of their output may be gathered from the circumstance that many thousand barrels are annually exported to the continental markets. A branch business is maintained at Yarmouth, where Messrs. Boston have similar premises and conduct a similar trade, this section of the enterprise being under the immediate control of Mr. Peter P. Boston. The concern has always been noted for the high quality and uniform superiority of the goods put forward. No pains are spared to secure the best catches in the first instance, and in order to carry out the work of curing, smoking, &c., under the most efficient auspices, various improved methods and processes have been adopted. Altogether the business may be fairly described as one of the largest and best organised connected with the east coast fisheries, and we have much pleasure in giving it due prominence in these columns. *Apropos* to the locality it may be mentioned that Messrs. Boston Brothers are extensive lessees of salmon fisheries.

### Mr. William Lyle, Dispensing Chemist, Hide Hill.

There is a spirit of progress abroad, some of our friends would call it destructive iconoclasm, which seems determined to leave no stone standing of the old traditional landmarks which were the beacons of our forefathers. Time was, and that till comparatively recent date, when the druggists' art and the dispensing of medicines, in the hands of the dispensing apothecary, was a slow, doubtful, and very often dangerous practice. How modern science and modern methods have altered all this! vegetables far beyond the possibilities of any published list. Among the chemists and druggists of Berwick-on-Tweed, Mr. William Lyle holds a leading and representative position. His business was established in 1880, and for fourteen years it has received the patronage of many of the best classes of residents in the town and district. The premises consist of an admirable double fronted shop on Hide Hill—a main thoroughfare running at right angles to the High Street. The arrangement of the place has been carried out with due regard to the requirements of a large and well established business. To the dispensing

EXTERIOR OF MR. W. LYLE'S PHARMACY.

INTERIOR OF MR. W. LYLE'S PHARMACY.

The chemist and drug dispenser of to-day is a man of education, thoroughly trained to his calling, fully acquainted with the whole pharmacopœia of British preparations, and having a knowledge of the properties of minerals and department the closest attention is given. The proprietor, having duly qualified by examination for this branch, may be relied upon for the care and precision which he gives to physicians' prescriptions and family recipes. The medical

# 1994

## UNIVERSAL BUILDING SOCIETY

### 1894 onwards

1897    William Lyle - chemist, druggist, photographic chemical and material dealer

1906    Edwin Erskine - chemist and druggist

1946    Edwin Erskine - chemist and druggist

1953    David M.Smith - photographer - 10 Hide Hill
         Universal Building Society - 12 Hide Hill

1962    Universal Building Society - 10/12 Hide Hill
         Fleming and Wood - agricultural merchants Office - 10/12 Hide Hill

On the closure of Edwin Erskine's dispensing chemist in the early 1950s, the premises were taken over by the Universal Building Society. The Building Society, based in Newcastle, has offices throughout North East England and the Borders where it offers customers flexible savings and investment accounts, mortgages and buildings and contents insurance. The Berwick branch employs five full time and one part time member of staff and the Manager is Graham Hush.

### Opening Hours

Monday, Tuesday, Thursday, Friday :        9.00 am to 5.00pm
Wednesday:        9.30 am to 5.00pm
Saturday:        9.00 am to noon

# 1994

## W. A. DOUGLAS AND PARTNERS

### 1894 onwards

1897    Adam Spaven - china dealer and furnishing ironmonger

1902    James Taylor Robson - ironmonger, china, glass and oil merchant and cycle agents - 12 - 18 Bridge Street

1925    James T.Robson - ironmonger - 7,12 + 14 Bridge Street

1936    J.T.Robson ( incorporated into W.C.Caverhill + Co.Limited ) - ironmongers

1938    W.C.Caverhill and Co. Limited - ironmongers

1962    Pram Shop

1975    Little Ones - "for complete baby layettes"

1978    Scarlet Ribbons - Ladies fashion shop

1984    John Sale and Partners - estate agents

1990    W.A.Douglas and Partners - antique and second hand furniture

W.A.Douglas and Partners, originally known as Squirrels, buys and sells antique and modern furniture and bric-a-brac. The business, owned by Mr Douglas, employs two full time and one part time members of staff and sells goods which range in price from 50 pence to £500.

**Opening Hours**
Monday to Saturday : 9.30 am to 4.00 pm

faculty and the general public repose the utmost confidence in the dispensing, and the large connection is undoubtedly the result of judicious management. The shop also contains a well selected stock of perfumes, medicated soap, combs and brushes, sponges, and all toilet and nursery requisites. These goods are of very superior character and in much request. Mr. Lyle has a department entirely devoted to the requirements of the photographic art, and we notice that he keeps a large stock of apparatus and is the only dealer in photographic materials in the town. Now that photography has become so popular and so essential in many ways, it is always desirable to be within easy access of a shop where one can purchase the various requisites with a feeling of confidence in their quality. Dry plates, chemicals, and complete apparatus are in stock and they have been obtained exclusively from the leading manufacturers in the country. Mr. Lyle is about to have a dark room fitted up on the premises for the use of his customers—a spirit of enterprise which will undoubtedly be highly appreciated.

### Mr. Adam Spaven, Ironmonger, 12 & 14, Bridge Street.

Despite the attractions of its walls, its gates, the Bell Tower and its Parish Church of Holy Trinity, Berwick, possesses no feature more striking than its old bridge over the Tweed. Having noted the somewhat marked disproportion existing between its 924 feet in length and its seventeen feet in width, the visitor will, in due course, turn away from the fifteen arches and proceed to stroll down Bridge Street. Amongst the earliest objects to attract him here will probably be numbered a display of fishing tackle, telescopes, field glasses, and other goods in the windows of the ironmongery establishment of Mr. Adam Spaven. This business was commenced forty years ago, and is now more than ever eminently adapted to meet the wants of its various customers. Situated within a few yards of the Corn Exchange, it is convenient for farmers and other frequenters of the Saturday markets. There is ample warehouse room at the rear and in the basement, as well as workshops for repairing purposes. Mr. Spaven displays stocks of travelling trunks, bonnet boxes and baths; field and opera glasses and telescopes; fishing tackle, including rods, reels, baskets, gaffs, landing nets, fittings, flies, etc.; clocks, china, tea sets, dinner services, electro plated goods, Southern and Richardson's Sheffield cutlery, for which he is sole agent. Also joiners' tools and an exhaustive stock of builders' ironmongery, including kitchen ranges, the "Vermont Convertible Range," decorative overmantels, brass and iron curbs for tile hearths, and such goods as bedsteads, bedding, and furnishing ironmongery generally.

12 AND 14, BRIDGE STREET.

## Mr. John Davidson,
### Grocer and Provision Dealer and Wine and Spirit Merchant, 111, 113, 115, and 117, High Street.

Napoleon's description of the English as a nation of shop-keepers was probably intended as a reproach, and has often been quoted as such, by writers possessed, let us say, of various degrees of wisdom. For our own part we are content to admit that we are a nation of shop-keepers, and we should go further, and observe that taking us all in all, no other nation in the world knows how to keep shop half so well or with half such good effect as we benighted inhabitants of this "right little tight little island." At all events it would prove a somewhat difficult task to instance a single English or Scotch town of importance in which really excellent shops do not exist, or in which (to put the case another way) businesslike enterprise has not been exerted to its utmost in order to provide the public with opportunities for doing their marketing under the most favourable and best conceivable auspices. Berwick is no exception to the rule, and in the well known establishment, or rather couple of establishments, to which we purpose devoting the present notice, she certainly possesses a grocery, provision, and wine and spirit emporium, such as would do no discredit to any centre of population in the country. Mr. John Davidson has occupied the premises in question ever since the year 1853. In 1871, however, they were entirely rebuilt and refitted, and now comprise two spacious, admirably arranged shops, the one used for the sale of groceries, provisions and Italian goods, and the other as a wine and spirit store. The first mentioned possesses a handsome double front, and extends rearward to a distance of about 70 feet, an additional 70 feet of warehouse accommodation being attached. The retail sales departments, both as regards the grocery and provision sides, have been fitted up in the most attractive modern style, and will be found to afford exceptionally comprehensive choice in all the best classes of comestibles and household sundries. A big array of tinned, potted, bottled and kindred delicacies also constitutes an important feature of the stock, the list of firms represented under these heads including every name of repute at present associated with the trade. In English, Irish, Scotch, Danish and American dairy produce of every description capital value is put forward, year in and year out. Quite a noteworthy line is made of home and foreign cheeses, and we may mention that last Christmas there was here to be seen a special Canadian cheese, weighing half a ton, or 1,120 lbs., all of which was sold within two days, being retailed in small quantities. The wine and spirit stores next door to the grocery establishment are arranged and equipped on a similar scale of completeness and efficiency. They include a handsomely fitted retail bar, together with order department, bottling stores, and capacious cellars stocked with the best qualities of liquors of all kinds. Over the main shop, which with the stores, runs back some hundred or more feet from the street, there is a further range of accommodation, also used for the purposes of the business. Blending and bottling operations are conducted on the premises, a circumstance which enables the proprietor to more readily ensure the character and condition of the beverages put forward; in fact, more carefully managed licensed premises do not exist in the neighbourhood. We need scarcely add that the valuable family and general trade embraces among its customers the principal families, hotels, etc., in Berwick and county. At the Low Green Rope Works, Mr. Davidson also carries on a successful business as a manufacturer of marquees, tents, rope, twine, nets, etc., and employs a number of hands in the making of salmon, herring and sheep nets, as well as ropes, twine and general cordage, mainly intended for farm use. A large marquee is available for hire, 100 feet long and 30 feet wide; this is largely used for the local Kettles, Picnics, and the meetings of the Militia, Volunteers, etc. The entire business well deserves the gratifying measure of support at present extended to it. By way of conclusion we may mention that Mr. Davidson ranks amongst Berwick's oldest and most highly esteemed public servants. For eighteen years he represented the North Ward in the Borough Council Chamber, retiring only some three years ago. He is also one of the Directors of the local Gas Company; a Director of the Benefit Building Society, and a Manager of the Berwick and Tweedmouth Savings Bank.

*111, 113, 115, AND 117, HIGH STREET.*

# 1994

## INTERSPORT

### 1894 onwards

| | |
|---|---|
| 1897 | John Davidson - grocer - 113 and 115 Marygate |
| 1902 | Renton and Co. - grocers |
| 1934 | Ralph Dodds and Sons Limited - grocers |
| 1953 | Dodds and Sons Limited - grocers |
| 1959 | The Kenya Cafe - James Scott and Son |
| 1978 | Ivor Scott and Co. - hardware, tools and gifts. |
| 1992 | Intersport - sportswear and equipment |

Intersport originally operated from premises in Castlegate but moved to Marygate in 1992. The shop sells a variety of sportswear and equipment for both indoor and outdoor sports including tennis rackets, footballs, running shoes and sports bags. Three full time and two part time staff are employed in the shop.

**Opening Hours**
Monday - Saturday :     9.00 am to 5.15 pm

**Goods Sold**
| | |
|---|---|
| Running Shoes : | £24.99 to £74.99 |
| Tennis rackets : | £12.99 to £99.99 |
| Hockey Stick : | £7.99 to £24.99 |
| Track Suit (adult) : | £29.99 to £49.99 |
| Walking Boots : | £29.99 to £110.00 |

## AULD BREWERS ARMS

### 1894 onwards

| | |
|---|---|
| 1897 | Brewers Arms Public House - 117 Marygate - John Davidson |
| 1902 | Brewers Arms Public House - Renton and Co. |
| 1925 | Brewers Arms Public House - Landlord : Matthew N. Kyle |
| 1934 | Brewers Arms - Landlord : Walter Pritchard |
| 1938 | Brewers Arms - Landlord : Joseph T. Davison |
| 1952 | Brewers Arms - Landlord : Dick Short |
| 1979 | Brewers Arms - Landlord : John Hynde |
| 1984 | Brewers Arms - Landlord : Douglas Rutherford |
| 1989 | Brewers Arms - Landlord : Billy Strachan |

The Brewers Arms, now known as Auld Brewers Arms has been in existence as a pub for nearly a century and its present landlord is Graham Phillips. The pub, which has a distinctive and unusual glass front, is known by locals as the "Battery". Two full time and four part time staff are employed there serving drinks and food.

**Opening Hours**
Monday - Saturday :     11.00 am to 11.00 pm
Sunday :     noon to 3.00 pm;
             7.00 pm to 10.30 pm

**Prices of Drinks**
| | |
|---|---|
| Lager (pint) : | £1.55 |
| Beer (pint) : | £1.50 |
| Wine (glass) : | £1.20 |
| Spirits (25ml): | £1.05 |

# 1 9 9 4

## TAIT SPORTS

### 1894 onwards

1897    Mrs John George Hickey - cabinet maker and upholsterer, undertaker and carpet warehouse

1902    Robert Kay Gaul - cabinet maker and upholsterer, undertaker and carpet warehouse

1910    Robert Kay Gaul - furniture dealer

1925    William Anderson and Sons - florist (23 Hide Hill )
        Robert Kay Gaul - cabinet maker (25 Hide Hill )

1934    William Anderson and Sons - florist (23 Hide Hill )
        Brown (W.S.), MacDonald and Fleming - chartered accountants (25 Hide Hill )

1969    William Anderson and Sons - florist and seedsmen.

1980    Eric Tait Sports

Tait Sports, now owned by Ann MacNab, has operated from these premises since 1980. The business sells sportswear, sports equipment and trophies. The shop employs two full time and four part time members of staff.

**Opening Hours**
Monday - Saturday :    9.00 am to 5.30 pm

**Goods Sold**
Trainers :          £19.99 to £79.99
Football Tops :     £24.99 to £36.99
Trophies :          £2.50 upwards
Bags :              £9.99 upwards
Footballs :         £4.99 upwards

### John G. Hickey, Artistic Cabinet Maker, Upholsterer, Undertaker, Valuer, &c., Hide Hill.

Artistic and general cabinet making finds excellent exemplification in the town in the central workshops of Mr. John G. Hickey, who is also largely engaged in the kindred lines of funeral undertaking, furniture removal and storage, valuation, house jobbing, etc. The business commands a wide connection, the proprietor being well known in the Border districts and a *persona grata* with all classes of clients. The undertaking was originated in Tweedmouth, in 1880, by the firm of Dickson and Hickey, and transferred to Berwick eight years later, Mr. Hickey, on the dissolution of partnership, which took place in 1893, purchasing his partner's interest in the concern. The premises enjoy the advantage of a good situation near the Town Hall, Post Office, Corn Exchange and the banks. They extend rearwards about ninety feet, and include a fine roof-lighted saloon for cabinet furniture and upholstery and furnishings of every description, this hall being fifty-five feet long and beautifully appointed and ordered. Further back are the cabinet and upholstery workshops, where exquisite suite and piece goods are made in all the favourite designs, and the best modern styles of upholstery illustrated; a large amount of repairs being also done. About twenty hands are employed by Mr. Hickey, and his leading productions are suites in all styles, cabinets, sideboards, cosy corners, piece cabinet work, bassinettes and mail carts. A complete assortment of the best modern furnishings is stocked with these, including beds and bedding, carpets, hearthrugs, floorcloths and drapery, so that buyers are able to select the complete outfit of a house of any size without trouble. Furniture is stored on easy terms, removals by road or rail carried out, decorative work and repairs to houses executed, etc. The undertaking department is also

HIDE HILL.

CABINET WORKSHOP.

44 BERWICK-ON-TWEED —ILLUSTRATED.

well equipped. Mr. Hickey is a valuer of all classes of property, and as he personally superintends the execution of all orders he is one of the busiest business men in Berwick, and commands general esteem and confidence.

## Mr. Nicol M. Craig,
### Dispensing and Family Chemist, 63, High Street.
### Telephone: No. 21.

Established in 1793 by the late Mr. W. Graham Carr, and subsequently carried on by his son, this high class dispensing and family chemists' business was acquired by Mr. Nicol M. Craig—fresh from a valuable experience of some considerable time with Messrs. Duncan, Flockhart and Co., and James Robertson and Co., of Edinburgh—when the shop, which possesses extensive and attractive frontages to both the High Street and West Street, was entirely re-modelled and modernised, and new plate glass windows put in. In the dispensing department, as being the most important, Mr. Craig gives strict and careful attention to the dispensing of physicians' prescriptions and family recipes entrusted to his care, and his scale of charges will be found as moderate as is consistent with the use of the best materials. The purity of all drugs, chemicals, and pharmaceutical preparations used in the compounding of medicines is also conscientiously guaranteed, no second quality of drugs being permitted on the premises. Among Mr. Craig's special preparations will be found his "Cydonia Cream" for summer and winter use, which not only produces a clear and beautiful complexion, but also removes roughness, redness, chaps, freckles, tan, and all other

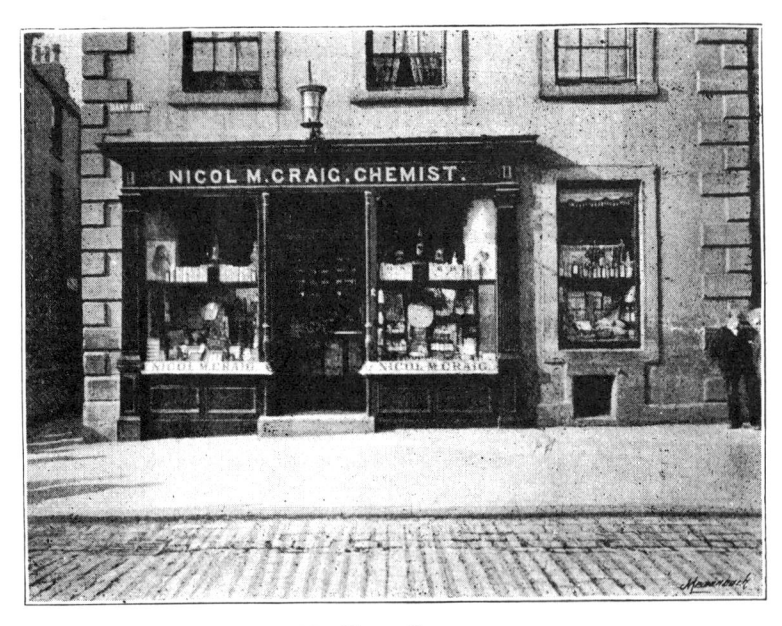

63, HIGH STREET.

INTERIOR OF 63, HIGH STREET.

# 1994

## GEORGE C. GRAY AND SON

### 1894 onwards

1897     Nicol Miller Craig - chemist

1920     James Rankine Hetherington - chemist and former assistant of N. M. Craig

1948     George C.Gray takes over business but still trades under name of J.R. Hetherington.

1953 - 1958     Name of business changed to George C. Gray.

c.1958     George C.Gray and Son

George C.Gray, a chemist originally from Grangemouth in Scotland, took over the premises from James Hetherington in 1948. Originally he ran the business alone, however, around 1958, his son, Robert, became a partner. When George retired, Robert then ran the business until his two sons, both qualified pharmacists, became partners - Andrew in 1986 and Steve in 1994.

Today the chemist's shop employs 3 full time staff as well as always having a pharmacist on duty. The shop dispenses prescriptions given by doctors under the National Health Service and sells various medicines, toiletries and health products.

In 1978 the family expanded the business and opened another chemist's shop in Main Street, Tweedmouth.

### Opening Hours

Monday - Saturday : 9 - 00 am to 5.00 pm

### Goods Sold

Cost of NHS Prescription : £4.75

# 1994

## GOVERNMENT SURPLUS STORES

### 1894 onwards

1897    Stuart Edington Simpson - baker and confectioner

1919    "Mr S.E.Simpson, Baker, Confectioner, etc. West Street begs to intimate that he is RETIRING FROM BUSINESS as at 29 November and . . . . . . that he will be succeeded by MR JAMES SCOTT, WOOLMARKET who has taken the whole over as a going concern . . . . ."

1934    Robert Scott - baker

1938    James Scott and Sons - bakers

1959    James Scott and Sons - bakers

1970    Government Surplus Store - proprietor Mr J.Peoples

1973    Government Surplus Store - proprietor Mr R.McGaw

1980    Government Surplus Store - proprietor Mr V.P.Moffat

These premises were used as a bakery for over a century before the Government Surplus Store opened here in 1970. The present proprietor is Mr Moffat who works in the shop. He sells government surplus clothes as well as workwear and camping equipment.

### Opening Hours
Monday - Saturday :    9.15 am to 5.00 pm
Half day closing on Thursday

### Goods Sold
Ex Army boots :        £30.00
Ex Army trousers :     £15.00
Sleeping Bags :        £13.00

blemishes of the skin, caused by hot sun, cold winds, frost, hard water, sea air, etc. It is undoubtedly a useful and valuable preparation, being really effective both as a preventive against and a remedy for the discomforts it is intended to counteract. Another speciality is the real Old English Lavender Water prepared by Mr. Craig. This particular distillation has long been a popular favourite alike on account of its agreeable perfume and its soothing and refreshing qualities in cases of headache, faintness, etc. It is, we believe, Her Majesty the Queen's favourite perfume, and is a standard article for toilet use. As prepared by Mr. Craig, we have a lavender water which possesses all the good qualities of the article to the full, it is highly fragrant and very lasting. In conclusion, we may state that in every department Mr. Craig's business bears the impress of the highest quality, and it is extensively supported by the leading medical men and private families in the district.

## Mr. S. E. Simpson, Baker and Confectioner, 38, West Street, Berwick-on-Tweed.

From some points of view the business of Mr. S. E. Simpson is one of the most important in Berwick, as his special and ordinary productions have come to be regarded as indispensable articles by a great number of the inhabitants. The business is one of old standing, having been founded in 1852 by Mr. Simpson's uncle, and has been developed by the founder and his enterprising successor with such success that it now takes the lead in the town, and enjoys a special place in public favour which is not a little flattering. The house enjoys an equal reputation in the matter of confectionery, pastry, and various specialities in household bread, everything made being superior in quality or possessed of special value from digestive power, palatableness, or superior nourishing qualities. *Inter alia* Mr. Simpson is celebrated for Scotch shortbread, Berwick cake, tennis cake, and a variety of pound cakes and pastry, for oatcakes and wine biscuit, the finest orange gingerbread, sweets, chocolates, and other toothsome comestibles. He is a specialist in the matter of wedding, christening, or birthday cakes, turning out the most artistic and ornate designs in these, but particularly in wedding cakes where his rare genius luxuriates in producing the most charming results. In what we may call more substantial articles, the chief place is held by Mr. Simpson's malt digestive bread, prepared according to Montgomerie's patent process, a method of preparation which has been almost universally recognised as the best, by experts as well as the public. This bread obtained the prize medal at the Edinburgh International Exhibition, 1886, and at the Glasgow Industrial Exhibition, 1886-7, was similarly distinguished, while private personages throughout the United Kingdom have borne ready witness to its good qualities. Dr. Wallace, Analyst for Glasgow, says : "The bread contains a large proportion of malt extract, together with whole meal and semolina. It has a fine fresh odour and agreeable taste, and will be found most acceptable to persons of weak digestion." From Windsor Castle comes the following under date 7th Dec., 1886 :—" Her Royal Highness Princess Christian desires me to express to you her very great satisfaction with the malt bread, biscuits, and rusks provided to her. Her Royal Highness considers them all very excellent.—Yours faithfully, Richard Tahourdin, Hon. Sec. to H.R.H. Princess Christian's Dinner Fund." As made by Mr. Simpson, this malt bread is of standard quality, and is in great favour in Berwick and the districts around. He also manufactures the "Hovis Bread," made from the germ of the wheat; it also commands an increasing sale, and as a digestive bread is highly recommended by the medical faculty; the "Health Bread," made from Seatree's Cumberland Brown Flour, which is a combination of several cereals; and also the ordinary wheaten bread, made in three different kinds—so that the most fastidious can procure a loaf suited to their taste. Malt biscuits we must not forget to note are also a leading speciality. Mr. Simpson's premises are centrally situated, and during his occupancy have twice undergone extensive alterations and

38, WEST STREET.

improvements, having now a lengthy, handsome shop frontage, the shop and windows of course full of the seductive specialities we have above indicated. The bakery occupies the rear, and is well up-to-date in its equipment. Among the mechanical appliances are some fine flour-sifting machinery, all flour being exhaustively sifted before being used. Then we observe the other machines for biscuits, cake-beating, dough-dividing, pie-raising, fruit-cleaning, peel-cutting, etc., all of which are of the most modern type for a hand power bakery. The trade is large and progressive, an important item being the catering for banquets, parties, etc., etc. The productions of the house are of excellent and uniform quality, and we do not hesitate to affirm that those forming business relations with it will find their interests guarded in every possible way under a policy of administration well calculated to ensure the mutual advantage both of vendor and buyer.

### The Hen and Chickens Hotel, Sandgate. Proprietor: Mr. J. E. Gray.

Few northern hotels are better known or enjoy a wider reputation for hospitality and good cheer, than the Hen and Chickens, Sandgate, Berwick. This famous hostelry has been in existence many years and was formerly conducted with great success by Mr. Erskine, who, however, retired some two months ago in favour of the present proprietor, Mr. J. E. Gray, a gentleman possessed of more than average *bon homie*, and who, prior to coming to Berwick, had fifteen years' experience of hotel management in "Auld Reekie," otherwise Edinburgh. The Hen and Chickens occupies an exceedingly central and convenient site almost adjoining the Corn Exchange. It has long constituted the rallying ground of the principal grain merchants, cattle dealers and other business men frequenting the Berwick markets; and for these as well as for "commercials" and general visitors, it affords exceptionally ample and comfortable accommodation. The billiard-room on the first floor is particularly worthy of note as being about the best equipped and certainly the best lighted apartment of the sort in the neighbourhood. The hotel is also well provided with the usual public and private rooms, stock-rooms, bars, smoke-room, bed-rooms, etc.—the whole being capitally furnished, and arranged with every regard for high class modern requirements. We need scarcely add that the *cuisine*, wine list, service and management are of an equally excellent character—the proprietor devoting careful personal attention to all details, and leaving no stone unturned to promote the well being and satisfaction of patrons; the old established prestige of the house seems little likely to suffer in his hands, and we may fittingly say in conclusion *siste, viator!* at any rate when you come to the Hen and Chickens!

THE HEN AND CHICKENS HOTEL.

### Messrs. Thomas Carter and Sons, Corn, Seed and Grain Merchants, Corn Exchange Buildings.

In association with the extensive agricultural district of which Berwick is the centre and chief market town, the granaries and stores of Messrs. Thomas Carter and Sons, corn and seed merchants, whose offices are in Corn Exchange Buildings, deserve mention. The business is one of the oldest in Berwick, having been established in 1837. Through its agency some thousands of quarters of grain, feeding stuffs and agricultural seeds change hands weekly. The granaries are in Sandgate, only a few yards from the Corn Exchange, convenient both to the Docks and the local markets. They contain ample capacity for the accommodation of large stocks of grain and other produce; and also a special plant of machinery for the manufacture of cattle food. Messrs. Carter and Sons are careful of their reputation and the various foods they supply are noted for high nutritive qualities, freedom from adulteration and meretricious ingredients and economical results. In selecting seeds they spare no pains in order to secure the best.

# 1994

## HEN AND CHICKENS HOTEL

### 1894 onwards

1897    Hen and Chickens Hotel . Proprietor - Lewis Small Hislop

1902    Hen and Chickens Hotel.  Proprietor - James Craig Pringle

1910    Hen and Chickens Hotel.  Proprietor - James Bolton Westle

1946    Hen and Chickens Hotel.  Proprietor - James Bolton Westle

1960s    Hen and Chickens Hotel.  Proprietors - Mr & Mrs Peter Foxton

1978    Hen and Chickens Hotel.  Proprietor - John Christie

1994    Hen and Chickens Hotel.  Proprietor - Ian Donaldson

The Hen and Chickens Hotel, situated in Sandgate near the Quayside, is an old coaching inn. It still operates as an hotel today, offering visitors a choice of 5 rooms.  The hotel is attached to the Scottish and Newcastle Brewery whose drinks are sold in the public bar. The business employs two people on a part time basis.

### Opening Hours

Monday - Saturday :   11.00 am to 11.00 pm
Sunday :   noon to 3.00 pm; 7.00 pm to 10.30 pm

### Prices

Pint of Beer :   £1.50 to £1.70
Food :   £2.00 to £11.00
Accommodation :   Bed and Breakfast £20.00 per person per night.

# ACKNOWLEDGEMENTS

The Borough Archivist wishes to thank the following people without whom this publication would not have been possible :

    Carole Wakenshaw for lending an original copy of the 1894 publication

    Jim Walker for all his patience and perseverance in taking the photographs

    Francis Cowe for providing research sources and information

    Linda Punton for typing the 1994 sections

    Edward Cawthorn, Chief Executive and Michael McDonald, Borough Planning Officer, of Berwick-upon-Tweed Borough Council for their support and ideas on presentation.


Berwick-upon-Tweed Borough Council gratefully acknowledge the following businesses who have supported this publication :

    B & M Motors

    Blackburn and Price Limited

    Clothesline Classic

    William Cowe and Son

    Crawfords Joinery

    W.A.Douglas and Partners

    George C. Gray and Son

    Hen and Chickens Hotel

    Ralph Holmes and Sons (Fish Merchants) Limited

    Kings Arms Hotel

    Paxton and Purves Limited

    Popinjays

    A & J Robertson (Granite) Limited

    Spar

    Edwin Thompson and Company